READ FOR REAL

Nonfiction Strategies for Reading Results

Authors

Leslie W. Crawford, Ed.D.
Professor of Literacy
Georgia College & State University

Charles E. Martin, Ph.D.
Professor of Early Childhood and Middle Grades Education
Georgia College & State University

Margaret M. Philbin, Ed.D.
Associate Professor Emerita
State University of New York Potsdam

Vocabulary and Fluency Consultant

Timothy V. Rasinski, Ph.D.
Professor of Education
Kent State University

English Language Learner Specialist

Caroline Teresa Linse, Ed.D.
Fulbright Scholar
Minsk State Linguistic University
Minsk, Belarus

Zaner-Bloser

Photo Credits

Covers: (wolves) Peter Weimann/Animals,Animals/Earth Scenes; (Machu Pichu) Robert Frerck/Getty Images; (lacrosse players) Michael Greenier Photography; (tomatoes) HWR Productions; (Amelia Earhart) Getty Images; (cowboy and steer) Tony Stone.

Models: George C. Anderson Photography

pp. 3, 70, Kent Dannen/PhotoResearchers, Inc; pp. 4, 80, 82(L), 83, 84, 88, Lawrence Migdale/Pix; pp. 5, 152, 159, Galen Rowell/CORBIS; pp. 8, 10(L), 11, Peter Weimann/Animals,Animals/Earth Scenes; pp. 9(L), 23, MarkStouferEnterprises/Animals,Animals/Earth Scenes; pp. 9(R), 13(L), 34, Mark Newman & Associates/ImageState; pp. 10(R), 15, Kirk Yarnell/ImageState; p. 12, John Giustina/GettyImages; p. 13(R), Tim Davis/PhotoResearchers, Inc; p. 14, Robert Winslow/Animals,Animals/Earth Scenes; p. 16, Charles Palek/Animals,Animals/Earth Scenes; pp. 22(R), 25(B), Gregory W. Brown/Animals,Animals/Earth Scenes; pp. 22(L), 26, Jeffrey Lepore/PhotoResearchers, Inc; p. 24, Nature's Images/PhotoResearchers, Inc; p. 25(T), Fritz Prenzel/Animals,Animals/Earth Scenes; p. 28, Stephen J. Krasemann/PhotoResearchers, Inc; pp. 32, 36, Scott Hanrahan/ImageState; p. 33, Ron Marretta/ImageState; p. 35, D. Robert and Lorri Franz/CORBIS; pp. 44, 53, Jeremy Horner/GettyImages; pp. 45(L), 64, Robin Smith/GettyImages; pp. 45(R), 69, George Ranalli/PhotoResearchers, Inc; pp. 46(R), 50, Robert Frerck/GettyImages; pp. 46(L), 49, 52, Mel Sauerbeck/Navaswan; p. 47, Harvey Lloyd/Helios; pp. 58(R), 59, 61, Haroldo de Faria Castro Cast/GettyImages; pp. 58(L), 60, 62, Hans Von Meiss/PhotoResearchers, Inc; pp. 68(R), 71(T), Mark Burnett/PhotoResearchers, Inc; pp. 68(L), 73(T), Mark Newman/PhotoResearchers, Inc.; p. 71(B), David Hiser/GettyImages; p. 73(B), Richard A. Cooke/CORBIS; pp. 81(R), 105, 116, 117(both), 118(L), 122, 124, 130(both), 131, 133, 134, 135, 136, 140(both), 144, 145, HWR Productions; pp. 82(R), 86(both), 142, Paul A. Souders/CORBIS; p. 85, Smithsonian American Art Museum, Washington, D.C./Art Resource, NY; p. 87, Michael Greenier Photography; pp. 132, 143, Zaner-Bloser, Inc.; p. 141, Martin Rogers/GettyImages; pp. 153(L), 168, FPGInternational; pp. 153(R), 154(L), 160, 176(both), 177(L), 178, 181, Hulton-Deutsch Collection/CORBIS; pp. 154(R), 156, Michael S. Lewis/CORBIS; pp. 155, 190(L), 195, CORBIS; pp. 158, 180, 189(R), 210(R), 214, 215, Bettmann/CORBIS; pp. 166(both), 170(both), 171, 172, 177(R), GettyImages; p. 167(I), Jeff Sherman/GettyImages; p. 167, Holmes-Lebel/FPG International; pp. 188, 196, National Cowboy Hall of Fame; pp. 190(R), 193, 194, Tony Stone; p. 212, Leonard de Selva/CORBIS; pp. 210(L), 213, Phil Schermeister/CORBIS

Art Credits

pp. 81(L), 94(both, 95, 98, 99, 101, Charles Shaw; pp. 96, 97, 104(both), 106–108, Kevin Brown; pp. 118(R), 119, 120, 123, Gershom Griffith; pp. 189(L), 191, 202, 203, 205, 206, Ed French.

ISBN 0-7367-2353-6

Zaner-Bloser, Inc., P.O. Box 16764, Columbus, Ohio 43216-6764 (1-800-421-3018)

Printed in the United States of America

05 06 07 08 (106) 5 4 3 2

Table of Contents

Table of Contents (continued)

Hi! We're your

READ FOR REAL
Reading Team Partners!

Have you noticed that the reading you do in science and social studies is different from reading stories and novels? Reading nonfiction <u>is</u> different. When you read nonfiction, you learn new information. We'll introduce you to some strategies that will help you read and understand nonfiction.

In each unit, you'll learn three strategies—one to use **Before** you read, one to use **During** your reading, and one to use **After** you read. You'll work with these strategies in all three reading selections in each unit.

In the first selection, you'll **Learn** the unit strategies. When you see a red button like this ⊚, read "My Thinking" notes to see how one of us used the strategy.

In the second selection in each unit, you'll **Practice** the strategies by jotting down your own notes about how you used the same unit strategies. The red button ⊚ will tell you where to stop and think about the strategies.

When you read the last selection in each unit, you'll **Apply** the strategies. You'll decide when to stop and take notes as you read.

Strategies

Here they are—the **Before, During,** and **After** Reading Strategies.

Use these strategies with all your nonfiction reading—social studies and science textbooks, magazine and newspaper articles, Web sites, and more.

Now that you've met the team, it's time to get started.

	BEFORE READING	DURING READING	AFTER READING
UNIT 1	**Preview the Selection** by looking at the title and headings to predict what the selection will be about.	**Make Connections** by relating information that I already know about the subject to what I'm reading.	**Recall** by summarizing the selection in writing or out loud.
UNIT 2	**Activate Prior Knowledge** by looking at the title, headings, pictures, and graphics to decide what I know about this topic.	**Interact With Text** by identifying the main idea and supporting details.	**Evaluate** by searching the selection to determine how the author used evidence to reach conclusions.
UNIT 3	**Set a Purpose** by using the title and headings to write questions that I can answer while I am reading.	**Clarify Understanding** by using photographs, charts, and other graphics to help me understand what I'm reading.	**Respond** by drawing logical conclusions about the topic.
UNIT 4	**Preview the Selection** by looking at the photographs, illustrations, captions, and graphics to predict what the selection will be about.	**Make Connections** by comparing my experiences with what I'm reading.	**Recall** by using the headings to question myself about what I read.
UNIT 5	**Activate Prior Knowledge** by reading the introduction and/or summary to decide what I know about this topic.	**Interact With Text** by identifying how the text is organized.	**Evaluate** by forming a judgment about whether the selection was objective or biased.
UNIT 6	**Set a Purpose** by skimming the selection to decide what I want to know about this subject.	**Clarify Understanding** by deciding whether the information I'm reading is fact or opinion.	**Respond** by forming my own opinion about what I've read.

Unit 1
Strategies

BEFORE READING

Preview the Selection

by looking at the title and headings to predict what the selection will be about.

DURING READING

Make Connections

by relating information that I already know about the subject to what I'm reading.

AFTER READING

Recall

by summarizing the selection in writing or out loud.

LEARN
the strategies
in the selection
Song at Nightfall
page 11

PRACTICE
the strategies
in the selection
Ghosts in the Twilight
page 23

APPLY
the strategies
in the selection
Hunters in the Shadows
page 33

Think About
the
Strategies

Preview the Selection

by looking at the title and headings to predict what the selection will be about.

My Thinking

The strategy says to look at the title and headings to predict what the selection will be about.

The title is "Song at Nightfall." The headings all seem to be something about wolves. I predict that this selection will be about wolves. Now I'm ready to read and see if I'm right.

DURING READING

Make Connections

by relating information that I already know about the subject to what I'm reading.

My Thinking

The strategy says to make connections by relating information that I already know about the subject to what I am reading. I will stop and think about this strategy every time I come to a red button like this ●.

Song at Nightfall

Wolves howling

It's just after dark near Yellowstone Lake in Yellowstone National Park. All is still except for the song of thousands of frogs. Then your ears prick up. A sound, starting low, then growing in loudness and rising in pitch, reaches your ears. The hair on the back of your neck stands up. A wolf is howling. Then another wolf joins in, and another. Soon the forest fills up with the **eerie** sounds.

Vo·**cab**·u·lar·y

eerie (**eer**•ee)—scary and mysterious

What Is a Wolf?

Wolves are mammals. A mammal is an animal that has hair, gives birth to live young, and feeds them milk. You are a mammal, too. So are mice, cats, and dogs. In fact, dogs and wolves are closely related. Thousands of years ago, humans came into contact with wolves and **tamed** some of them. They may also have taken in lost wolf pups. However it happened, wolves became **domesticated**. Humans were able to use them to help with work.

Over time, dog species were developed from the wolves. Siberian huskies, Alaskan malamutes, and German shepherds are dog species that look and act a lot like wolves. Wolves and dogs are both **carnivores**. Carnivores are animals that eat meat. The biggest difference between dogs and wolves, though, is that wolves are wild. They don't depend on humans for any of their needs. Wolves will become unhappy if they cannot roam free.

Gray wolf announcing its location

Gray Wolves and Red Wolves

Two kinds of wolf are found in North America: the gray wolf and the red wolf. The gray wolf is larger. The males can weigh as much as 150 pounds. There are many types of gray wolf. The main difference among them is the color of their fur. The arctic wolf, even though it is white, is a type of gray wolf. So are the wolves living in Yellowstone National Park. Gray wolves are northern wolves. They live in Canada and in states that border Canada, such as Minnesota and Idaho. Red wolves are smaller. Males may reach 80 pounds. Red wolves live in the southwest United States and in Mexico. And they are being **reintroduced** in North Carolina. In the past, both species lived in much larger areas.

Wolves of North America

Strategy

Make Connections by relating information that I already know about the subject to what I'm reading.

My Thinking
I knew that the red wolves and the gray wolves had some things in common. I also knew there were differences between them. This chart helps me relate what I already know about these animals to what I'm reading in the rest of this selection.

Red Wolf
(Scientific name: *Canis rufus*)

Range (where they live)
Southwest United States, Mexico; reintroduced in North Carolina

Color
Red, gold, brown, reddish-brown

Weight (males are usually heavier than females)
60–80 pounds

Size
2–3 feet at the shoulder

Prey (what they eat)
Rodents, small mammals, deer

Status
Endangered in U.S.

Gray Wolf
(Scientific name: *Canis lupus*)

Range (where they live)
Northern United States, Canada, Alaska; reintroduced in Idaho, Montana, Wyoming

Color
Black, gray, white; often a mix of these

Weight (males are usually heavier than females)
80–150 pounds

Size
3–4 feet at the shoulder

Prey (what they eat)
Rodents, deer, elk, bison

Status
Endangered throughout U.S. except for Minnesota; no need for protection throughout Canada

The Pack That Hunts Together Bunks Together

Wolves hunt together in groups called packs. When chasing a large animal like an **elk,** the wolves may space themselves out across a long distance. One wolf starts the chase. Then, as it gets tired, another wolf takes its place. The wolves stay in touch with each other with barks and cries. Eventually, the elk cannot run any more, and the wolves will kill and eat it.

Just as the members of the wolf pack hunt together, they also live together. A pack usually has 2 to 20 members. A pair of wolves called the **alpha** wolves—the alpha male and the alpha female—leads the pack. Many of the pack members are related to the alpha pair. They may be sons, daughters, sisters, brothers, or grand-children of the alphas. The alpha wolves usually stay together for their whole lives. They are also usually the only members of the pack that have pups.

An alpha male shows another wolf that he's the leader.

Help With the Pups

Although the alpha pair has the pups, the whole pack helps raise them. The pups are born in April or May, just when the weather starts to get warmer. The alpha female finds a narrow cave or ledge in which to give birth. The cave is called a den. The pups stay in the den for the first few weeks of their lives, nursing from their mother. The

A mother wolf carries her pup.

rest of the pack brings food to the mother during this time. This way, the pups are never left alone. Many other animals might find the wolf pups to be a good dinner, so it is important to protect them.

Gradually, the pups start to eat meat. Pack members bring food for them. They eat meat on a hunt and bring it in their stomachs. Then they **regurgitate** the partially digested food for the pups. Some pack members, usually aunt or uncle wolves, baby-sit the pups. They take care of the pups so the alpha female can hunt with the pack. Pups are not full-grown until they are two years old. The pack needs the strong alpha female to return to hunting as soon as she can, so a baby-sitter wolf has a very important job.

Finding a Place in the Pack

As the pups grow, they learn how to hunt. They also learn about their place in the pack. Each wolf in a pack knows exactly which wolf is more important and which wolf is less important. The alpha wolves are the most important. Then there might be a **beta** wolf, the next wolf in line. A few wolves never seem to join a pack or start one of their own. They are called lone wolves.

Vo•cab•u•lar•y

regurgitate (ree•**gur**•ji•tayt)—to bring up partially digested food

beta (**bay**•tuh)—the second letter of the Greek alphabet; the wolf next in line to the lead wolf in a wolf pack

Strategy

Make Connections by relating information that I already know about the subject to what I'm reading.

My Thinking

I didn't know that wolves wagged their tails, and I didn't know they wrestled. But it said that wolves were a lot like dogs, and I've seen dogs doing these things.

Sniff, Wrestle, and Howl

The members of a wolf pack develop close **bonds** and take care of each other. They communicate well, using their excellent senses of touch, smell, hearing, and sight to get their messages across. Wolves are smart and curious, and they are able to share their knowledge with other pack members. They mark their territory and other interesting places with scents. They recognize each other by sniffing and making sounds.

Wolves also communicate with their bodies. The tail alone can tell a lot about a wolf's place in the pack and how it is feeling. A wolf with its tail curled around its body is a lower-ranked wolf. A wolf that holds its tail high is a higher-ranked wolf. Wolves also wag their tails the way dogs do. Wolves lick, touch, and wrestle to play and to claim their place in the pack. The wrestling may look like fighting, but wrestling wolves don't usually hurt each other.

Vo·cab·u·lar·y

bonds (bonds)—feelings of loyalty and affection

Wolves bark, whimper, and growl. They also howl. Hearing a pack of wolves howling in full voice is an eerie experience. The sound can sometimes be heard for miles. Wolves howl to announce their location to other members of their pack and to other packs. They can hear other packs from as far as 10 miles away.

Howl Around the Campfire

Howling seems to help the pack members have strong ties to each other. And, just as humans enjoy a good sing around the campfire, wolves seem to enjoy a good long howl! The howling of wolves is a scary sound to people. People often think 20 or more wolves are howling when it is really only 6 or 8. That's one of the reasons people have been afraid of wolves, even though healthy wolves have never been known to attack a person. Wolf **conservationists** believe these beautiful animals are to be respected, not feared. Sometime if you're out camping and you hear wolves howling, gather around your own campfire and join in the song!

Vo•**cab**•u•lar•y

conservationists
(kohn•sur•**vay**•shuh•nists)—
people who work to protect wildlife

Think About the Strategy

AFTER READING

Recall
by summarizing the selection in writing or out loud.

My Thinking

The strategy says I should recall by summarizing the selection in writing or out loud. I can do this by telling the main parts of what I read. I learned that wolves are animals that live in packs. The wolves in the pack help each other get food and raise pups. There are two main types of wolves in the United States. Wolves and dogs are a lot alike, and they are smart and curious. Each wolf knows its place in the pack. Wolves should be respected, not feared.

Graphic organizers help us organize information. I think this article can be organized by using a web. Here is how I organized the information. I put my central idea in the circle in the very middle. I used the main ideas in the four main circles attached to the middle circle. I put details about the main ideas in the circles attached to each of the main circles.

Web

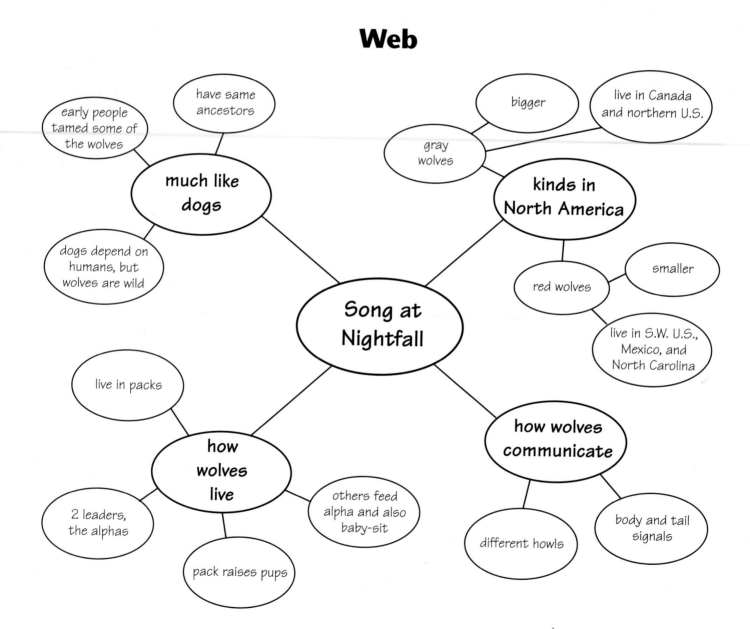

I used my graphic organizer to write a summary of the article. Can you find the information in my summary that came from my web?

A Summary of
Song at Nightfall

Wolves and dogs are much alike because they have the same ancestors. Long ago, people tamed some wolves and called them dogs. Today, some dogs still look a lot like wolves. Dogs have learned to depend on humans, but wolves are wild and roam free.

The two kinds of wolves in North America are the gray wolf and the red wolf. Gray wolves are bigger and live in Canada and the northern United States. Red wolves are smaller and live in the southwestern United States, Mexico, and North Carolina.

Most wolves live together in packs. Each pack has two leaders, the alpha male and the alpha female. They are the strongest pair and often are the only pair that has pups. Their pups are raised by the whole pack. Other wolves bring food for the alpha female and her growing pups, and they baby-sit so she can hunt with the pack.

Wolves bark, whimper, growl, and howl to communicate with each other, especially while they hunt together. They howl to show they are part of a pack and to tell the others where they are. Wolves use their bodies and tails to show their importance in the pack. The alpha male and female hold their tails high. Other wolves in the pack might curl their tails around their bodies.

So pay closer attention to the sounds your dog makes. When he howls, he might just be remembering his wild past.

Introduction
Here is my introduction. It tells what I will write about. The main idea is in the center of my web.

Body
I used information from each main circle and its details for each paragraph in my body copy.

Conclusion
I summarized my paper by recalling the main ideas.

Developing Vocabulary

Suffixes

A word part can give you a clue about a word's meaning. A **suffix** is a word part at the end of a word. A suffix adds to the meaning of a word root.

The suffix *-ist* means "a person who does, makes, works, or believes." "Song at Nightfall" contains the word *conservationist,* which means "a person who works to protect or conserve wildlife."

Here are more words with the suffix *-ist* and their meanings.
 artist – a person who makes art
 pianist – a person who plays the piano

On a separate sheet of paper, match each job title and its correct meaning. If you need help, use a dictionary. Then write three more words with *-ist* and give their meanings.

1. naturalist
2. scientist
3. environmentalist
4. biologist
5. physical therapist

a. a person who studies living things
b. a person who studies plants and animals in nature
c. a person who heals muscle injuries by special exercises
d. a person who studies the physical world through experimentation
e. a person who works to improve the condition of the natural world

Poetry

Wolf pups are important to the whole pack. This poem tells about the daily life of a wolf pup. Read the poem several times. If possible, practice it with a partner or a small group. When you are ready, read it to the class.

Fluency TIP

As you practice the poem, be sure to emphasize the singsong rhythm and rhyme in your voice.

The Wolf Pup's Song

When I was first born,
I stayed close to Mother.
I nursed and snuggled
With sisters and brothers.

I'm still just a pup;
I stay close to the den.
I want to go hunt.
I must ask my dad, "When?"

He says when I'm two;
'Til then I'll be yearning.
From aunts and uncles,
I'll try to keep learning.

Your place in the pack
Is important to know.
Close to each other,
Together you'll go.

That's what Aunt Nell says.
She's our baby sitter.
She watches and feeds
All pups in the litter.

Wolves have a good life.
We wrestle and we play.
We live in the wild,
And together we stay.

We howl in the night.
We don't mean to scare you.
It's just how we say
We like living near you.

Think About the Strategies

BEFORE READING

Preview The Selection

by looking at the title and headings to predict what the selection will be about.

 Write notes on your own paper to tell how you used this strategy.

DURING READING

Make Connections

by relating information that I already know about the subject to what I'm reading.

 When you come to a red button like this ●, write notes on your own paper to tell how you used this strategy.

Ghosts in the Twilight

A professional hunter/trapper

The trapper took off his snowshoes. Crossing the floor, he placed a pile of gray pelts onto the counter. (Pelts are the skins of animals.) "I brought in twelve pelts," the trapper said. "Pay up the **bounty,** please!"

For many years, the United States government offered a bounty on wolves. People thought that wolves killed sheep and cattle and might also attack people. People feared wolves and hunted them with the goal of stamping them out.

The bounty, plus the fear, worked well. By 1950, wolves had disappeared from most of the lower 48 states. It was a **twilight** of the wolves.

Over time, and on their own, wolves are returning to some areas. Many gray wolves live in Canada. They have been moving south. They are coming into northern Michigan, Minnesota, and other border areas. But wolves are still absent from most of the places where they lived in the past.

Vo•**cab**•u•lar•y

bounty (**bown**•tee)—a payment for killing a certain animal

twilight (**twy**•lyt)—a period of decline

[23]

Threatened, Endangered, Extinct

Many life forms on Earth are in trouble. People keep moving into more areas of the earth. Then the life that already lives there has three possibilities. One is to learn to live with people. For example, many birds easily live in neighborhoods.

Another option is to move. Sometimes, though, there is no place to move. For example, people have been building houses along the beaches. But an animal that lives on the shore may not be able to move inland.

A third possibility is that the **species** may become **extinct**. Extinct means that no more animals of that kind are alive.

Each species has a special role to play in its community. Losing a species through extinction is a loss for the whole community it lived in. That's why scientists and governments get involved.

Scientists have come up with two names for species that are in trouble. They may be **endangered** or they may be **threatened**. Endangered species are in serious trouble. They could become extinct if steps aren't taken to save them. When a species is threatened, it needs to be protected.

One endangered plant is the Nellie Cory Cactus.

Vo•cab•u•lar•y

species (spee•sheez)—particular type of animal or plant

extinct (ik•stingkt)—no longer living or existing

endangered (en•dayn•juhrd)—in danger of becoming extinct

threatened (thret•nd)—at risk of becoming endangered

The American alligator is no longer endangered.

We tend to think of animals, birds, and fish when we think of endangered species. But many species of plants are also endangered or threatened. In many cases, these plants provide the food for animals. If one species becomes extinct, its loss can cause problems for many other species.

The Endangered Species List

Scientists decide if a species is endangered or threatened. **Lawmakers** decide if the species goes on the endangered list. Usually, the lawmakers discuss the species with scientists. Then they follow their advice to make the decision. They list names of all the species that are protected by law in the United States.

The manatee is another endangered animal.

Vo·**cab**·u·lar·y

lawmakers
(**law**•may•kuhrz)—people, such as senators and representatives, who are elected to offices and make laws for a country

[25]

The law is called the Endangered Species Act. It was passed in 1973. It tells how species are chosen for the list and how they are to be protected. It also gives the **penalties** for harming a listed species. The U.S. **Environmental** Protection Agency keeps track of the list.

Once a species is put on the list, a plan is made to protect it. Its number is checked often. If the plan works, the number goes up. The species may be delisted, or removed from the list. An example of a delisted species is the American alligator. American alligators were almost extinct. They were put on the endangered species list. There is a **healthy** number of alligators today. When scientists found that the species was no longer threatened, they delisted it.

What About Wolves?

Are wolves endangered? Under U.S. law, they are. The number of wolves inside the lower 48 states is very small. But outside our country's borders, it's a different story.

Vo·cab·u·lar·y

penalties (**pen**•uhl•teez)— punishments, often in payment of a fine

environmental (en•vy•ruhn•**men**•tl)—having to do with Earth's natural resources

healthy (**hel**•thee)—large enough to keep the species alive

A gray wolf pack in winter

Canada never gave bounties for wolves. Healthy numbers of wolves live there, so gray wolves in Canada are not in danger.

In efforts to return gray wolves to places where they once lived, like Yellowstone National Park, scientists made a plan. In 1995, they decided to safely and legally catch some of the Canadian gray wolves. After caring for them for several months near the wolves' new home in Yellowstone, the scientists were able to turn them loose. These were the first wolves to live free in the area since the early 1930s. There are now several hundred gray wolves in the Yellowstone area.

The reintroduction of gray wolves in the park has been a big success. The animals have been returned to their natural habitat, and their numbers are growing. Gray wolves are no longer in danger of becoming extinct. In general, they do not need legal protection as an endangered species does. But because they had all but disappeared in the U.S., gray wolves were placed on the endangered species list in 1973. In fact, they were among the first animals to be protected by the Endangered Species Act.

So the placement of Canadian gray wolves in Yellowstone brings up a new question. Is a species protected because of what it is or because of where it lives?

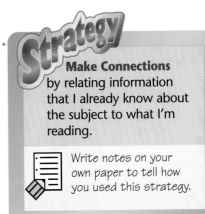

Strategy

Make Connections by relating information that I already know about the subject to what I'm reading.

Write notes on your own paper to tell how you used this strategy.

Natural Versus Introduced

Suppose that a Canadian wolf crosses over the border into Montana. It is endangered in the U.S., and it is protected. But the wolves in Yellowstone are not completely protected. They did not move into Yellowstone on their own. They were brought in from an area where their numbers were good. So those wolves are not endangered.

Thus, a wolf that kills farm animals may be shot—but this is true only if it is one of the reintroduced Canadian wolves. A **natural** wolf is completely protected. Anyone killing a wolf that is in the area on its own could be arrested and punished.

How do you tell the natural gray wolves from the introduced gray wolves? It's hard. Court cases are trying to answer this question. It is hoped that a **compromise** can be reached.

Vo·cab·u·lar·y

natural (**nach**•uhr•uhl)—there on its own or by nature

compromise (**kom**•pruh•myz)—an agreement in which each side gets and gives things it wants

[27]

Red wolves are also the focus of **controversy**. In the wild, red wolves were nearly extinct. There were only 14 of them left. People were able to capture these wolves. The captured wolves were kept in protected places, and their numbers increased. Some of the offspring are being released into their former ranges, such as North Carolina. Red wolves, however, are still protected under the Endangered Species Act.

Questions About the Future of the Wolves

The future of the gray wolves in Yellowstone is still in doubt. Packs are settling into their new homes there in the park. But they may still be removed. Farmers and ranchers fear livestock losses. And Canada will not take the wolves back. If they are removed, the gray wolves will either be killed or placed in zoos. There are no easy answers.

Vo·cab·u·lar·y

controversy (**kon**•truh•vur•see)—a situation in which different opinions are strongly held

A red wolf being reintroduced into North Carolina

The American Wolf—Endangered or Not?

Natural Wolves	Introduced Wolves
A Canadian gray wolf that crosses the border into the United States is considered endangered.	A Canadian gray wolf that is introduced in the United States by humans is not considered endangered.
A Canadian wolf that crosses the border into the United States is completely protected by law.	A Canadian wolf that is introduced into the United States by humans may be shot if it kills farm animals; it is not completely protected by law.
There are no "natural" red wolves in North Carolina, so all red wolves there are considered endangered.	All red wolves in North Carolina were reintroduced there, so they are completely protected by law.

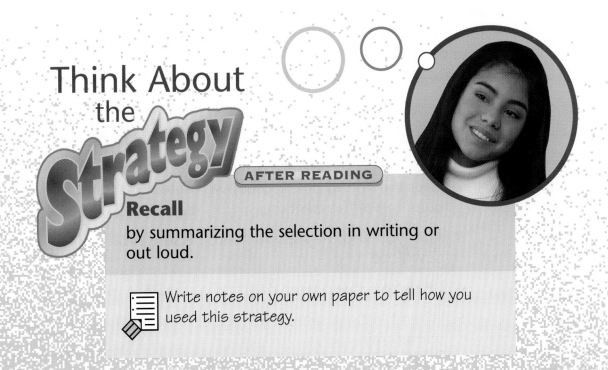

Think About the Strategy

AFTER READING

Recall
by summarizing the selection in writing or out loud.

Write notes on your own paper to tell how you used this strategy.

Vocabulary

Compound Words

Compound words are words made from two or more smaller words. To figure out the meaning of a compound word, separate it into two words. The meanings of the smaller words often help you understand the compound word.

Lawmakers is a compound word from "Ghosts in the Twilight." *Law* and *makers* are the two smaller words. *Lawmakers* means "people, such as senators and representatives, who are elected to offices and make laws for a county."

Here are two more compound words from the article:
snowshoes = *snow* + *shoes* ("webbed frames that attach to boots or shoes for walking on the snow without sinking")
Yellowstone = *yellow* + *stone* ("a place with yellow stones")

Read the sentences below. Find the compound word in each one. On a separate sheet of paper, write the compound words. Next to each word write the two smaller words that make the compound word. Write what you think each word means. Then compare your answer with the definition in a dictionary.

1. The order from the general came directly from his headquarters.

2. After the voting polls closed, we waited for the outcome of the election.

3. After you find the file you need, be sure to download it.

4. Cows and sheep were part of the rancher's livestock.

5. When I lost the same book again, I felt like a scatterbrain.

News Report

Protecting endangered animals is a topic you often hear about on the news. With a group, assign parts and practice reading this radio news report. When you are ready, present the report to the class.

Fluency TIP

Try to imagine yourself as a character in this short play. Read your part as you think the character might really say the lines.

Mayor Asks for Respect for Endangered Wolves

Reporter: In the northern border town of Hinkley, Minnesota, Mayor Jane Greene called a news conference today to discuss the rumors of wolf sightings outside the town. The mayor began with this statement:

Mayor: Yesterday, Conservationist Edward George of the U.S. Fish and Wildlife Service confirmed the rumors. He told me that the Service estimates that nearly 60 wolves are living in our county. They are endangered. Therefore, it is illegal to disturb, injure, trap, or kill the wolves.

Reporter: Some local folks have expressed fear about their new neighbors. Jack Aron, a farmer, said:

Jack Aron: "I don't want those wolves to mess with my land!"

Reporter: And Karen Hick, a teacher worried about the safety of her students, had this to say:

Karen Hick: "Can I let the children go outside to play, knowing there are wolves out there?"

Reporter: Mayor Greene encouraged residents not to fear.

Mayor: We need to learn about wolves.

Reporter: Conservationist Ed George added to the mayor's comment.

Edward George: We believe that wolves do not bother humans if humans do not bother them. They won't go after children or domestic animals. Wolves are essential to the ecosystem. We must do what we can to let them live in peace.

Reporter: Stay tuned for further developments.

Think About
the
Strategies

BEFORE READING

Preview the Selection
by looking at the title and headings to predict what the selection will be about.

DURING READING

Make Connections
by relating information that I already know about the subject to what I'm reading.

AFTER READING

Recall
by summarizing the selection in writing or out loud.

Use your own paper to jot notes to apply these Before, During, and After Reading Strategies. In this selection, you will choose when to stop, think, and respond.

HUNTERS IN THE SHADOWS

Snow geese

The ranger puts the walkie-talkie to her mouth. She pushes down the button. "We're all ready here. All quiet," she says in a quiet voice. She takes one more look around the fenced pen. The dark green fir trees whistle softly in the early morning breeze. Snow geese, headed north, cross the clear blue sky. A whisper comes over the walkie-talkie. "On my mark—three, two, one, now!"

The ranger focuses her **binoculars** on the animals on the far side of the snow-covered, acre-wide pen. The pack is resting, but alert. They know something is going on. Slowly, a section of fence is rolled back. The largest of the gray-black animals pricks its ears. Then it stands. Carefully, it goes to the opening in the fence. It sniffs all around the opening. It peeks outside and then is gone. The ranger wipes away a tear. For the first time in 50 years, wolves are free in Yellowstone National Park.

Vo·cab·u·lar·y

binoculars
(buh•**nok**•yuh•luhrz)—a hand-held instrument used with two eyes to make faraway things look closer

[33]

Return of the Wolves

Until a few years ago, the sight and sound of gray wolves was missing from Yellowstone. Park workers were trying to return Yellowstone to the way it was in the early 1800s. That was before many people visited the area. They succeeded in bringing back almost every species but one. There were no wolves. The park was like a jigsaw puzzle with one piece missing. In 1995, wolves were reintroduced, or brought back, to Yellowstone. Now Yellowstone could be seen as a finished puzzle again.

A Yellowstone elk

Role of Wolves

An **ecosystem** is made of all the living and nonliving things in a certain area and their **interactions**. Every part of an ecosystem is important. Plants use sunlight, air, water, and parts of the soil to make food. Some animals, such as grasshoppers and elk, eat the plants. Other animals eat animals. Finally, there are animals and bacteria that eat dead or decaying stuff. In a healthy ecosystem, each species eats or is eaten! When one part of the chain is missing, the system is upset.

Wolves are **predators**. In Yellowstone in the past, wolves ate large animals, such as **bison** and elk. They also ate smaller animals, such as mice. When the wolves were gone from Yellowstone, the number of elk rose. They ate plants faster than the plants could grow back. The elk became hungry and sick. Predators such as wolves were needed. Wolves tend to attack and kill sick or injured elk. This helps keep the elk

Vo·cab·u·lar·y

ecosysytem (ek·oh·sis·tuhm)—the plants, animals, and nonliving things that make up an environment and have an effect on each other

interactions (in·tuhr·ak·shuhnz)—the ways things work together

predators (pred·uh·tuhrz)—animals that live by hunting and eating other animals

bison (by·suhn)—large, shaggy-headed mammals living in the western United States

herd healthy. It also helps keep the number of elk from growing faster than the plants do. Wolves help keep the ecosystem of Yellowstone balanced.

Wolf Arrivals

The wolves that were returned to Yellowstone were found in Canada. They were given drugs to make them sleep. Then they were flown to their new home in the park. For the first few months, the wolves lived in a large pen. About an acre of land was fenced in at several places. This gave the wolves time to recover from their trip. They got used to their new home.

The wolves didn't hunt. Instead, park employees fed them. They gave the wolves the **carcasses** of animals found within the park. This is the same food they hoped the wolves would hunt when they were free. Finally, in January 1995, the gate was opened. The wolves were free.

Gray wolf with a carcass

Vo•**cab**•u•lar•y

carcasses (**kar**•kuhs•ez)— dead bodies

For and Against the Wolves

Many people are happy that the wolves have been returned to Yellowstone. Others, though, have a different view. They oppose returning the wolves for many reasons. The issue is complex.

One Side of the Coin

For many people, the day the wolves were freed was a wonderful day. They were excited about truly **restoring** the ecosystem in the park. They felt as if they were making up for all the wolves that had been needlessly killed for bounty in the 1800s.

A hungry wolf

Many people, too, are worried about the number of species that are becoming extinct. Many scientists think that for a natural area to be healthy, it should have **biodiversity**. Biodiversity is the number of different species in an area. Wolves were very nearly extinct in the United States. Restoring wolves to Yellowstone will let the species live on.

Another Side of the Coin

Other people were upset that the wolves were brought back to Yellowstone. Ranchers had cattle and sheep grazing near the park. They were worried that the wolves would not stay inside the park's borders. They feared that the wolves would kill livestock. The managers of the wolf project tried to set up rules for handling wolves that killed farm animals. But many ranchers were still concerned.

Other people who were against the reintroduction of the wolves believed that it should be allowed to happen naturally. They thought that lone wolves that sometimes made their way south from Canada should be allowed to move into the park on their own and start packs. It might take many decades, but wolves would return to Yellowstone on their own.

Vo·cab·u·lar·y

restoring (ri•stor•ing)— returning something to the way it was

biodiversity (by•oh•di•vur•si•tee)—the variety of plants and animals growing in a certain area

Forming Your Own Opinion

Returning wolves to Yellowstone has caused a lot of controversy. Both sides have strong **opinions**. They also have good points to make. Most people form opinions according to their values.

Values are the things you think are important. What are your values? How do they affect your opinion about the wolves in Yellowstone?

The first paragraph of this article makes you want to root for the wolves. But what if it had described a hard-working rancher finding a valuable calf that had been killed by wolves? It's important to try to see both sides of a question. Then you can decide for yourself.

Opinions About Returning Wolves to Yellowstone National Park

For	Against
It will keep the elk at healthy numbers and protect the plant life.	Farm animals will be killed.
It improves the biodiversity (the number of different species in an area).	Reintroduction doesn't let nature take its own course.
It returns Yellowstone to the way it was 150 years ago.	Other ways to control the number of elk are just as good as reintroducing wolves.
It returns wolves to the United States much earlier than they would return on their own.	The wolves will not stay inside the boundaries of the park.
It allows visitors to the park to have experiences with wolves.	If the reintroduction doesn't work, the wolves will be killed or put in zoos.

Vo•**cab**•u•lar•y

opinions (uh•**pin**•yuhnz)— decisions about which side is right in an argument or controversy

Context Clues

Context clues can help you figure out the meaning of an unknown word. First, look at the words near the unknown word. Then reread the sentences nearby. You will find clues to the word's meaning.

Read the following passage from "Hunters in the Shadows."

> *The ranger focuses her **binoculars** on the animals on the far side of the snow-covered, acre-wide pen. The pack is resting, but alert.*

Use context clues to find the meaning of *binoculars*. The word *focuses* tells you the ranger adjusted the binoculars to see something more clearly. The words *animals* and *far* tell you that the ranger used the binoculars to look at animals at a distance.

Together, the clues suggest that *binoculars* are instruments used to see things more clearly at a distance. The second sentence, which supports that suggestion, describes what the ranger saw.

Read these passages from "Hunters in the Shadows." Use context clues to help you find the meanings of the words *predators* and *carcasses*.

> *The elk became hungry and sick. **Predators** such as wolves were needed. Wolves tend to attack and kill sick or injured elk. This helps keep the elk herd healthy.*

> *Instead, park employees fed them. They gave the wolves the **carcasses** of animals found within the park. This is the same food they hoped the wolves would hunt when they were free.*

On a separate sheet of paper, write your definitions of the words *predators* and *carcasses*. Then write the clues that helped you find the meaning of each word.

Readers' Theater

In this Readers' Theater, a wolf cub and an alpha male wolf are about to be set free in a new place. A narrator helps set the stage. Read over the play several times, taking turns playing different parts. When you are ready, present the play to the rest of the class.

Fluency TIP

Practice this script with two other people. Help one another read the script with appropriate expression and feeling.

We Need to Be Free

Narrator: In January 1995, the Canadian wolves that were brought to Yellowstone National Park were reintroduced into the wild. They had spent several months living in an enclosed space, getting used to their new home.

Wolf Cub: Papa, what's going on? There are people moving the fence. Something must be happening!

Alpha Male Wolf: Yes, I see it, too. Something *is* happening.

Wolf Cub: I hope they don't make us move again. I was just starting to like it here!

Alpha Male Wolf: Yes, me too. It hasn't been easy, adjusting to this new place. We all miss our home in Canada.

Wolf Cub: Do the people mean well, Papa? They do give us shelter and feed us so we don't starve. That's good, isn't it?

Alpha Male Wolf: Yes, the people do treat us well. But we shouldn't have food handed to us. We are born hunters. Our instincts tell us what to eat and when to hunt for our own food. We need our own space. We need to be free.

Wolf Cub: Oh! Look! That person is rolling back the fence. Are we being set free?

Alpha Male Wolf: I don't know. I'll find out. You stay here.

Narrator: Alpha Male Wolf runs over to the fence. He sniffs and peeks beyond the opening. Then he quickly runs off.

Wolf Cub: Hey! Papa ran beyond the fence. He's free! Mama! Brothers! Sisters! We're free!

READING
in the Real World

Schedule

Suppose you want to watch a television program that will tell you more about wolves. A program schedule is a handy tool for finding shows you want to watch and the times they will be on the air.

Monday, September 27	4	6	10	28	34
4:00 PM	Birthday Zoo	Young and Wild: The Dating Game	Dog Days	Barking Mad: Series 2	Barking Mad: Series 2
4:30 PM	Animal Allies	That's My Baby: Mojo		Breed All About It: Beagles	Breed All About It: Rottweilers
5:00 PM	Amazing Animal Videos	Amazing Animal Videos	Amazing Animal Videos	Amazing Animal Videos (Season II)	Amazing Animal Videos (Season II)
5:30 PM	Vets in Practice: Blood, Sweat, and Tears	Vets in Practice: Love Is All Around	Vets in Practice: Trouble Ahead	Vets in Practice: Langford Revisited	Vets in Practice: Series 1, episode 1
6:00 PM	Pet Project: Gate Wide Shut	Pet Project: The Wizard of Paws	Pet Project: Who Shot Daisy?	Pet Project: Marking Our Territory	The World of Horses With John Scott: The Three-Day-Eventing Horse
6:30 PM	Into the Wild: Humpbacks of Hawaii	Animal Tracks: Swimming With Salmon, Whales	Into the Wild: Wolves and Caribou	Animal Tracks: California Crows, B.C. Porpoises	Into the Wild: Santa Cruz Island
7:00 PM	Nikon Wildlife Expeditions: Cubs in the Canopy	Nikon Wildlife Expeditions: N. America's Big Five	Nikon Wildlife Expeditions: Coastal Rain Forest Black Bears	Nikon Wildlife Expeditions: Feeding Humpback Whales	Profiles of Nature: Growing With Nature
7:30 PM	Animal Hospital: Series 9	Animal Hospital: Series 9	Animal Hospital: Series 102	Animal Hospital: Series 10	Nick's Quest: Crocodiles
8:00 PM	The Planet's Funniest Animals (Season IV)	Crocodile Hunter Diaries (Season II): Dancing With Devils	Jeff Corwin Experience (Season II): Brazil: The Amazon Goin' Bananas	Meerkats Unmasked	Pet Star
8:30 PM	K9 to 5: Cadaver Dogs, Sled Dogs				

Discussion Questions

Answer these questions with a partner or on a separate sheet of paper.

1. Compare this television schedule to a calendar showing one month. How are the schedule and the calendar the same, and how are they different?

2. A show about wolves and caribou will be shown on Channel 10 at 6:30. What show comes on after that one?

3. You also like to watch shows about dogs. What are three shows that might interest you?

4. Which show below can you watch after school and before dinner, between 4:00 and 5:30?

    a. Into the Wild: Humpbacks of Hawaii
    b. Animal Allies
    c. Nikon Wildlife Expeditions: Coastal Rain Forest Black Bears
    d. Nick's Quest: Crocodiles

5. Which of the shows below is the longest?

    a. Pet Star
    b. Pet Project: Marking Our Territory
    c. Into the Wild: Santa Cruz Island
    d. Animal Hospital: Series 9

6. How can you tell that some shows on this schedule are repeats?

7. Would "Vet's World" be a good title for this whole series of shows?

    a. Yes, because the shows describe what a vet does.
    b. Yes, because some shows are called "Vets in Practice" and "Animal Hospital."
    c. No, because only some of the shows describe what a vet does.
    d. No, because some shows are about funny animals.

8. Which statement best describes the people who like to watch these kinds of shows?

    a. They are mostly adults.
    b. They are mostly children and teenagers.
    c. They have many pets.
    d. They care about animals.

EXPLORE MORE

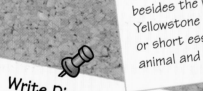

Bulletin Board Display

Carry out research to prepare a bulletin board display of dogs that look and act a lot like wolves. Include pictures or illustrations of the dogs and brief descriptions of modern characteristics of each one.

Animals in Danger

Check with a reference librarian or search on the Web to find information on animals that have been classified as threatened, endangered, or extinct. Choose one animal and develop a chart or a larger display that shows the animal and tells where it lives or describes its habitat. Include additional information, such as its main foods and any special or unique physical features or social behaviors.

Yellowstone Wildlife

Find books or Web sites about Yellowstone National Park and learn more about this unique place in the United States. Choose an animal besides the wolf that makes Yellowstone its home. Write a story or short essay that describes the animal and its everyday life in the park.

Wolf Debate

Choose whether you are "for" or "against" bringing wolves back into Yellowstone National Park. Make a list of reasons for your choice. Then prepare an argument to present to the class. Be sure to include facts in your presentation, not just your opinions. Try to convince your classmates that your choice is the best choice.

Write Diary Entries

Imagine being a park ranger or a wolf conservationist. Write several diary or journal entries that trace a pack of wolves just reintroduced into the wild. Identify and describe each member of the pack, starting with the alpha wolves. Tell about behaviors the wolves exhibit, such as hunting, caring for pups, and communicating with one another in various ways.

My Life as a Wolf

Pretend that you are a wolf, either one in a pack or a lone wolf. Write a story about your everyday life. Tell what your life is like, and describe how you communicate with other wolves.

Related Books

Evert, Laura. *Wolves*. NorthWord Press, 2000.

Greenberg, Daniel A. *Wolves*. Benchmark Books, 2003.

Gresko, Marcia S. *Wolves: Nature's Predators*. KidHaven Press, 2003.

Gunzi, Christiane. *The Best Book of Wolves and Wild Dogs*. Kingfisher Publications Plc, an imprint of Houghton Mifflin Company, 2003.

Kalman, Bobbie, and Amanda Bishop. *The Life Cycle of a Wolf*. Crabtree Publishing Company, 2002.

Leach, Michael. *Wolf*. Steck-Vaughn Company, 2003.

Martin, Patricia A. Fink. *Gray Wolves*. Children's Press, 2003.

Spilsbury, Richard and Louise. *A Pack of Wolves*. Reed Educational & Professional Publishing, 2003.

Interesting Web Sites

Defenders of Wildlife This site offers information on how to protect wildlife.
http://www.defenders.org/atrisk/

Help Save the Wolves Check out this site to learn how you can be involved in wolf conservation.
http://www.savewolves.org/

International Wolf Center This site contains articles, photos, and information about wolves, and links to the center's wolf study program.
http://www.wolf.org/wolves

Kid's Rendezvous Site: Information on Wolves This kids' site about wolves has information about wolves, activities, and a booklist.
http://www.timberwolfinformation.org/kidsonly/kidsonly.htm

Mission: Wolf Here is a wolf education center that has permission to keep wolves.
http://www.missionwolf.com

National Wildlife Federation This site has numerous links to features and information about wildlife, ecology, and conservation.
http://www.nwf.org

Wolf Park This is another site from a wolf conservation and education center. It has links to photos of individual wolves as well as other interesting information.
http://wolfpark.org/

Yellowstone Wolf Reintroduction This site gives the history of the reintroduction of wolves into Yellowstone National Park and the current status of the wolves.
http://www.forwolves.org/ralph/historical.html

Unit 2
Strategies

BEFORE READING

Activate Prior Knowledge

by looking at the title, headings, pictures, and graphics to decide what I know about this topic.

DURING READING

Interact With Text

by identifying the main idea and supporting details.

AFTER READING

Evaluate

by searching the selection to determine how the author used evidence to reach conclusions.

LEARN
the strategies
in the selection
The Someday That Never Came: Machu Picchu
page 47

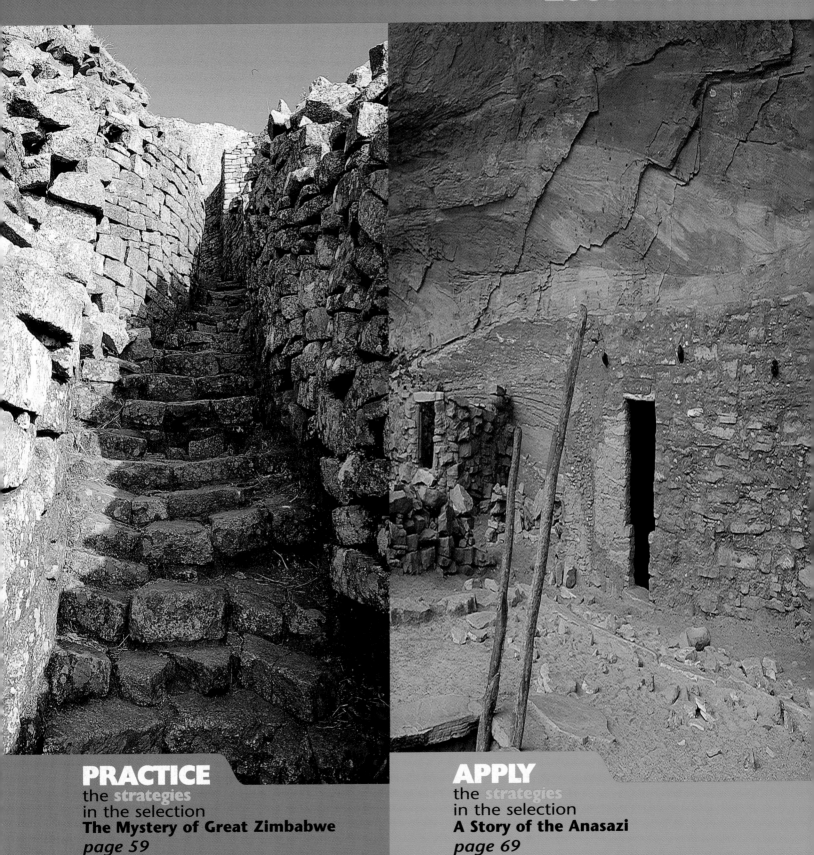

PRACTICE
the *strategies*
in the selection
The Mystery of Great Zimbabwe
page 59

APPLY
the *strategies*
in the selection
A Story of the Anasazi
page 69

Think About
the
Strategies

BEFORE READING

Activate Prior Knowledge
by looking at the title, headings, pictures, and graphics to decide what I know about this topic.

My Thinking
The strategy says to look at the title, headings, pictures, and graphics to decide what I know about this topic. The title and all the headings say something about "Machu Picchu." All the pictures show scenes from that place. They look like the place is up high in the mountains. A chart shows how high some places are above sea level. I read about Machu Picchu in a *National Geographic* magazine. I remember that it's in the Andes Mountains, and it's hard to get there.

DURING READING

Interact With Text
by identifying the main idea and supporting details.

My Thinking
The strategy says to interact with text by identifying the main idea and supporting details. I will stop and think about this strategy every time I come to a red button like this ⦿.

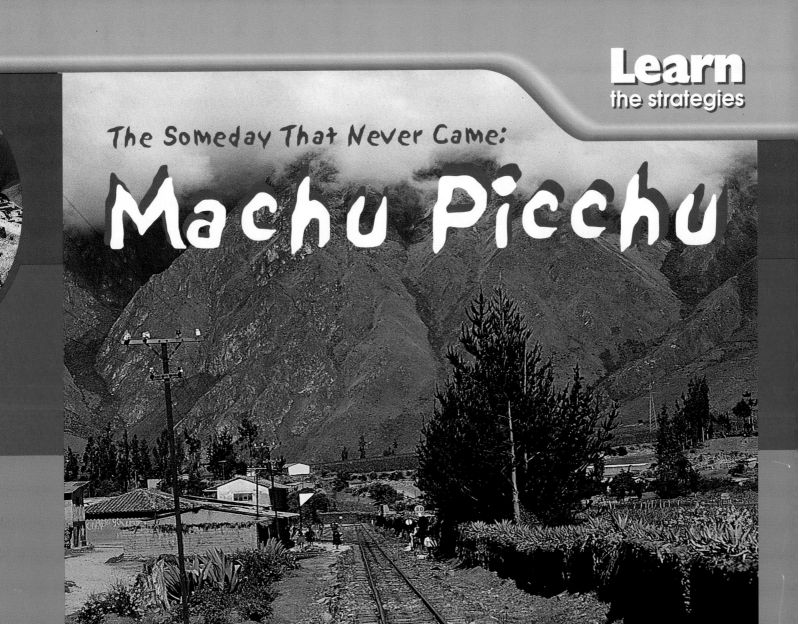

The Someday That Never Came:
Machu Picchu

Train station along the way from Cuzco, Peru, to Machu Picchu

The train climbed higher and higher, round and round, straight up! It came from **Cuzco,** many miles back. Now the road was getting steeper and steeper. Rachelle and her family were high up in the Andes [**an**•deez] Mountains on their way to **Machu Picchu**.

Rachelle looked out one side of the train and then the other. She looked up ahead as best she could. But it only looked to her as if they were going up the steepest mountain she had ever seen! It looked as if they were on a train to the clouds. But they were on a train to an Inca city built hundreds of years ago.

Rachelle pulled on her dad's sleeve. "Dad, are you sure we're on the right train?" she asked. "It looks as if this train is going nowhere!"

Vo•**cab**•u•lar•y

Cuzco (**koo**•skoh)—a city in Peru

Machu Picchu (**mah**•choo **peek**•choo)—an ancient city built by the Inca

[47]

Strategy

Interact With Text by identifying the main idea and supporting details.

My Thinking

The main idea here is that Incas built stone roads in the Andes Mountains. Details are that the roads went to all parts of the empire, they helped the people send messengers quickly, they helped trading, and they helped the army move quickly.

"Don't worry, Rachelle. We're on the right train. We have many more hours to travel, though. After we leave the train, we still have a long bus ride." Her dad peered out of the train window, too. "It's just that Machu Picchu is a very hard place to get to. That's why no one found it for so long." He went on to tell Rachelle about the mystery of Machu Picchu.

What Was Machu Picchu Like?

Back in the 1400s, one of the groups of people who lived in Peru was the Inca [**ing**•kuh]. By the 1400s, they ruled much of South America west of the Andes Mountains. These mountains rise steeply along the west coast of South America. The Inca built stone roads all through them. The roads were very important to their empire. They helped the Inca send messengers quickly to all parts of the empire.

These stone roads helped them move important trade goods. Things such as food, cloth, and gold could go from one place to another pretty easily. These roads also helped the Inca army move quickly. That was important for two reasons. First, it helped keep the empire strong. And second, it helped the rulers make sure their people were taken care of and safe.

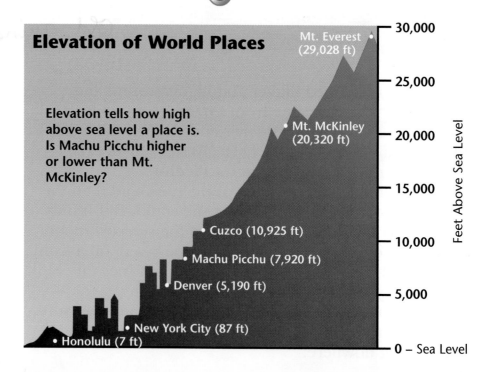

Elevation of World Places

Elevation tells how high above sea level a place is. Is Machu Picchu higher or lower than Mt. McKinley?

Feet Above Sea Level

- Mt. Everest (29,028 ft) — 30,000
- 25,000
- Mt. McKinley (20,320 ft) — 20,000
- 15,000
- Cuzco (10,925 ft) — 10,000
- Machu Picchu (7,920 ft)
- Denver (5,190 ft) — 5,000
- New York City (87 ft)
- Honolulu (7 ft) — 0 – Sea Level

The rulers took a part of everything that was made by the people, grown by the people, and taken out of the ground by the people. This included tons of gold and emeralds. In return, the rulers made sure the people were protected.

The Inca rulers were **pagan** religious leaders, too. Part of their job was to make sure that their gods were kept happy.

The rulers also asked the people to spend some time each year working on public projects such as buildings and roads. The main road, now called the Inca Trail, was built very well. Many parts of it are still used today.

Some of the ruins at Machu Picchu

Often, the distance between towns was long. Then the Inca built inns and resting places, just like roadside rest stops along the highways in the U.S. The Inca probably started to build Machu Picchu around the middle of the 1400s. Some people think it was built just as one of those resting places along the Inca Trail.

Vo·cab·u·lar·y

pagan (**pay**•guhn)—not from one of the main religions; relating to the worship of many gods

Strategy

Interact With Text
by identifying the main idea and supporting details.

My Thinking
The main idea is that Machu Picchu may have been a city or a vacation spot for rich Incas. Supporting details say the stone buildings were made with great skill, and there are many large homes or palaces.

Machu Picchu was probably more of a city than a simple resting place along the road. The stone buildings were put together with great skill. The stones that were used to form the buildings do not all have square corners. In fact, one stone was carefully carved with 37 angles. It **aligned** perfectly as a corner with many other stones.

The question is, "Would that much art, effort, and skill be put into a roadside rest stop?" Also, several large homes, or palaces, are found at Machu Picchu. This leads some people to think that the city may have been a vacation spot for wealthy Inca people.

There is an unusual building with three large windows. It was built along one side of the city. No other Inca building in all of Peru has three windows or windows that large. This building may have been used to check the position of the sun in the sky. So some people think Machu Picchu might have been built as a special place to hold religious ceremonies.

Machu Picchu ruins, with Huayna Picchu Mountain in the background

Vo·cab·u·lar·y

aligned (uh•**lynd**)—arranged or lined up in a special way

[50]

Machu Picchu: Lost

We believe that people lived in Machu Picchu until the early 1500s. Spanish invaders conquered the Incas in the middle 1500s. But the city was already **deserted**. No one knows why the city was built. And no one knows why it was deserted. It may have been too hard to get up to, perched high in the Andes between two mountain peaks.

Some scientists think the water ran out. The water in Machu Picchu was supplied from underground springs. Maybe they dried up.

Whatever the reason, Machu Picchu was deserted many years ago. It's strange, but this desertion is what saved the city in the long run. The Spanish army destroyed the Inca empire. They killed many people and took away the riches.

But the Spanish army never found Machu Picchu. It was high in the misty Andes Mountains. Through Machu Picchu's wonderful buildings with windows and doorways, we get just a glimpse of this once-thriving culture and its skills in art and building.

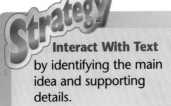

Strategy

Interact With Text by identifying the main idea and supporting details.

My Thinking
I think the main idea here is that the Spanish army never found Machu Picchu. They would have destroyed it, like they did the rest of the Inca empire.

Machu Picchu: Found

For hundreds of years, Machu Picchu sat empty. Trees took root in the wide **plazas**. Roofs thatched with grass caved in. Birds nested in the **niches** in the massive stone walls. By the early 1900s, only a few people living high in the Andes still knew about the lost city. You'd never find it on your own. You had to know where to look.

That's when Hiram Bingham arrived. Bingham was a history teacher from Yale University. He was looking for the lost Inca city of Vilcabamba [vil•kuh•**bahm**•buh]. Bingham studied papers written by Spanish people in the 1500s. He thought the city would be somewhere northwest of Cuzco. In 1911, with the help of a local guide, he found Machu Picchu instead.

The trail to Machu Picchu zigzagged back and forth. Had it gone straight up, it would have been very dangerous. At one point, Bingham and his group had to cross a narrow rope bridge. It swayed over a deep canyon. Bingham's group realized they would have to build better bridges and roads before they could really explore Machu Picchu. Otherwise, they would not be able to bring the equipment and gear they needed up to the city.

Vo•cab•u•lar•y

deserted (di•**zur**•tid)—left empty; abandoned

plazas (**plah**•zuhz)—public squares

niches (**nich**•ez)—ledges cut into walls where statues can be displayed

Strategy

Interact With Text
by identifying the main idea and supporting details.

My Thinking
The main idea is that Machu Picchu is a big tourist attraction. It took a long time, but people cleaned up the place and published pictures about it. This made tourists want to go there.

Over the next several years, Bingham led teams that **excavated** the city. (He led teams that found Vilcabamba, too.) They removed dirt, rock, and plants that had grown up over the stone. They returned toppled stones to the tops of walls. They made drawings and took photographs. These were published in *National Geographic*.

Now everyone could see the fountains, stairways, and terraces of Machu Picchu. Everyone could see how its plazas, palaces, and temples were laid out. Today, Machu Picchu is the most popular tourist attraction in Peru.

Terraces at Machu Picchu

Machu Picchu: Mystery

"Dad, what's that path with the backpackers on it?" Rachelle pointed out the window.

"That's the old Inca Trail," he answered. "It takes backpackers 5 or 6 days to reach Machu Picchu on it."

Her dad's voice got softer. "Imagine climbing the Inca Trail 500 years ago. A dozen **llamas** trail out behind you. You're carrying corn or maybe expensive weavings for an

Vo·cab·u·lar·y

excavated
(ek•skuh•vay•tid)—uncovered; exposed to view

llamas (lah•muhz)—South American animals related to camels; used to carry things

Inca prince. The city is noisy and bustling with activity when you arrive." His voice got softer still. "Then imagine that you are the last one to leave. Imagine leaving the empty, silent city behind. You move lower and lower on the mountain until the city is lost in the mist . . ."

"Yes." Rachelle picked up the story. "Maybe you hoped you'd be back someday—a someday that never came."

Part of the Inca Trail in Cuzco, Peru

Think About the Strategy

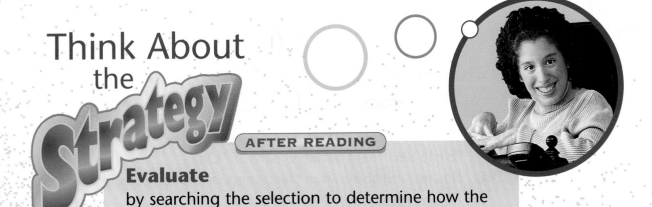

AFTER READING

Evaluate

by searching the selection to determine how the author used evidence to reach conclusions.

My Thinking

The strategy says I should evaluate by searching the selection to determine how the author used evidence to reach conclusions. The writer concludes that the Inca Trail was built very well, because parts of it are still being used. Machu Picchu's buildings were put together with great skill, because the stones were carved and fitted together perfectly. The Spanish army didn't find Machu Picchu, because it's still standing. Machu Picchu is a favorite tourist attraction because Bingham and his team cleaned it up well and had drawings and pictures published in *National Geographic*.

An outline shows the main points and the supporting details of the paragraphs in a piece of writing. Every letter and numeral in the outline stands for something in the summary. Words or sentences that are shown with Roman numerals represent entire chunks of the summary. Items shown with capital letters and numerals represent main ideas and supporting details.

Outline

The Someday That Never Came: Machu Picchu

I. Introduction
    A. Machu Picchu is high in the Andes Mountains.
    B. It was built by the Incas.
    C. It is a mystery.

II. Body
    A. What was Machu Picchu like?
        1. It was connected to other places by stone roads.
        2. It may have been a resting place along the Inca Trail.
        3. It may have been a vacation spot for wealthy Inca people.
        4. It may have been a special place to hold religious ceremonies.
    B. Machu Picchu became lost.
        1. People lived there until the early 1500s.
        2. No one lived there when the Spaniards came in the middle 1500s.
        3. No one knows why it was deserted.
        4. It was safe because it was well hidden in the mountains.
    C. Machu Picchu is found again.
        1. Hiram Bingham studied papers written by Spanish people in the 1500s.
        2. He looked for one place, but he found Machu Picchu instead.
        3. Getting there was very difficult.
        4. He and his teams made drawings and took photographs.
        5. Machu Picchu became a tourist attraction.

III. Conclusion
    A. Machu Picchu is high up in the mountains and is very hard to get to.
    B. It is a popular place for tourists.
    C. They try to guess what happened there long ago.

I used my graphic organizer to write a summary of the article. Can you find the information in my summary that came from my outline?

A Summary of
The Someday That Never Came:
Machu Picchu

Machu Picchu is a mystery. The Incas built this city high in the Andes Mountains. Still, no one is certain why they built it.

Introduction
I used the information under Roman numeral I to write the introduction.

Machu Picchu is on the Inca Trail. The city might have been a resting place. It could have been a vacation spot. Maybe religious ceremonies were held there. No one knows for sure.

For some reason, the Incas deserted this city in the early 1500s. The Spaniards invaded the Inca empire in the middle 1500s. However, they never found this city. It was well hidden in the mountains.

In 1911, a history teacher was looking for a different Inca city. His name was Hiram Bingham. He found Machu Picchu instead, but it was not easy. Bingham and his team followed a trail that zigzagged through the mountains. They studied the city. They drew and took pictures of what they saw. Then many people learned about Machu Picchu. They wanted to see it.

Body
I used information under Roman numeral II in my outline for the body of my summary. The information under each capital letter became the paragraphs in this part of the summary. The numerals under each main idea list my supporting details.

Now this city is a very popular place to visit. Tourists walk through the area. They imagine how the city looked long ago. They try to guess why the Incas left and never came back.

Conclusion
I summarized my paper by using information under Roman numeral III.

Words Borrowed From Spanish

Many English words are borrowed from other languages. The word *plaza* in "The Someday That Never Came: Machu Picchu" is borrowed from Spanish. *Plaza* means "a public square."

Sometimes when you know the origin of a word, it is easier to remember the meaning of the word. Then you can use borrowed words from Spanish in your own writing to make a story more interesting.

Look at these English words that are borrowed from Spanish.

> *stampede*—a group of animals or people moving quickly in the same direction
>
> *tornado*—a violent funnel of wind

Read this list of words that are borrowed from Spanish. On a separate sheet of paper, write a sentence for each word. For extra challenge, write sentences that include two of the words.

1. **renegade**—a person who does not follow laws
2. **armada**—a large group of battleships
3. **rodeo**—a sporting event that includes bronco riding and calf roping
4. **lasso**—a rope with a loop at the end for catching cattle and horses
5. **embargo**—an order from a government that stops another country from exporting goods

Readers' Theater

With a small group, assign parts and practice reading the script below. When you are ready, perform it for the class. Practice saying these Inca names until you can read them aloud easily.

Chilche [**cheel**•cheh], Tiso [**tee**•soh], Tanqui [**tahn**•kee]

Fluency

TIP

Try to capture the feelings of the characters in your voice as you practice and present this script.

Going Up But Never Coming Back

Narrator: Listen to Rachelle and her father tell about the Inca Trail to Machu Picchu.

Father: Imagine, Rachelle, that you're walking this path 500 years ago. Feel how hard it is to breathe? That's because we're up so high in the mountains.

Rachelle: Look! The llamas don't seem to be having any trouble at all. But I'll bet they're glad they don't have to walk straight up the trail either.

Father: Yes, the Inca builders who made this trail really knew what they were doing. They built the trail in a zigzag pattern. That way, travelers don't have to climb straight up the steep path.

Narrator: Listen as Father helps Rachelle pretend they are on a journey to Machu Picchu long ago. They plan to meet with other family members when they arrive.

Father: You may be getting tired from climbing, but you're excited, too. Your cousins will already be there, waiting for us.

Rachelle: (laughing) You mean my cousin who is an Inca prince?

Father: Yes, your cousin Prince Chilche and his younger brothers, Tiso and Tanqui. Maybe we should stop to rest for a few minutes. We can check the bundles the llamas are carrying.

Rachelle: Yes, those beautiful weavings are pretty, and they are so heavy to carry. But we'll be arriving at the busy, beautiful city very soon now. The city in the clouds is so magical!

Father: Enjoy yourself, Rachelle, because we'll have to leave soon after we arrive so we'll have time to get back down before sunset.

Rachelle: We're not even there yet, but I'm already planning to return to Machu Picchu next year!

Narrator: Yes, Rachelle and her family will be starting the journey down soon. The clouds and a cool mist will follow them. And Rachelle is planning their return next year. But those are plans that will never happen.

Think About the Strategies

BEFORE READING

Activate Prior Knowledge

by looking at the title, headings, pictures, and graphics to decide what I know about this topic.

Write notes on your own paper to tell how you used this strategy.

DURING READING

Interact With Text

by identifying the main idea and supporting details.

When you come to a red button like this ⊙, write notes on your own paper to tell how you used this strategy.

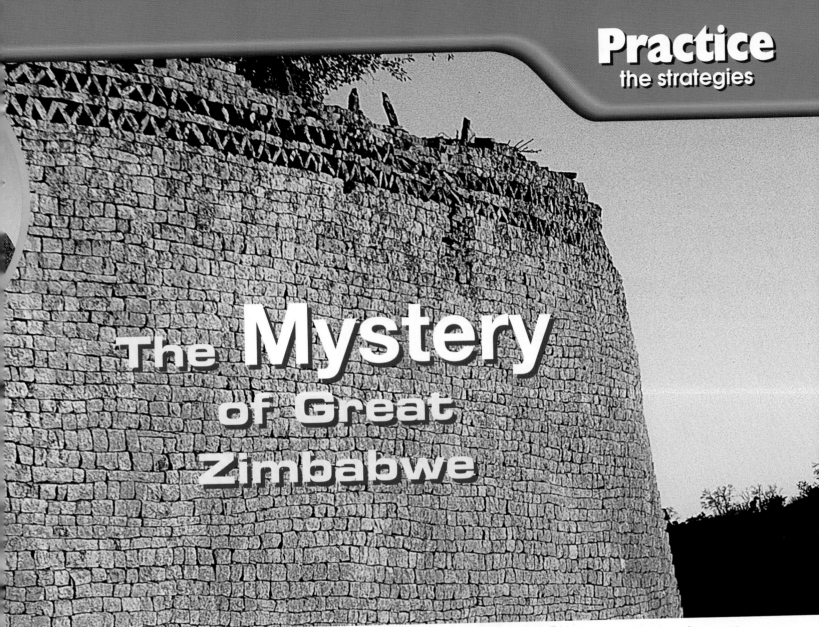

The Mystery of Great Zimbabwe

The Great Enclosure at Great Zimbabwe

As soon as the car stopped, Tony climbed out of the back seat. It had been a long drive to **Great Zimbabwe** from **Harare**. He was eager to look around. The sky was brilliant blue. All around, low trees grew in clumps of deep green in the yellow-gold grasses. The landscape was beautiful, but it wasn't what captured Tony's attention. Right in front of Tony rose a huge white stone wall. It stood out brightly against the wide, open space he and his parents had driven through.

Great Zimbabwe is what remains of the capital city of a great kingdom that ruled southeast Africa from about 1200 until about 1450. All that's left now is the strongest parts of what was built. These strongest parts are great

Vo•cab•u•lar•y

Great Zimbabwe (grayt zim•**bahb**•way)—a very old city in the country of Zimbabwe

Harare (huh•**rar**•ay)—the capital city of Zimbabwe

[59]

granite walls that enclose two main areas and piles of stone that show where other **enclosures** used to be.

The Great Enclosure

"This is the Great Enclosure we talked about in the car, Tony," his dad said. "Do you remember what the guide-book said about how the walls were built?"

Tony ran his hand over the wall. "I can see now what the book meant." He traced the line between two stones with his finger. "The stones fit together exactly, without any mortar to stick them together." Tony peered closer. "It's so tight I can't even get my fingernail between these two stones."

The tower of Great Zimbabwe

Vo•cab•u•lar•y

granite (**gran**•it)—a very hard stone used for building

enclosures (en•**kloh**•zhuhrz)—spaces surrounded (closed in) by a fence or walls

Tony looked up. The stone wall towered over him. That made him think of the tower. "Let's go inside the walls, Dad. I want to see the tower."

Tony and his dad went through an opening in the thick double walls into a large oval-shaped area. Sections of walls were broken down, and there were piles of rubble. When the Great Enclosure was first built, there were walls inside. The walls separated the space into different areas. At one end were a platform and a round tower that had no doors and no windows.

"Dad, what was that tower used for?" Tony asked. "You can't go in. You can't get out."

"No one knows, Tony," his dad answered. "It's about 34 feet tall—about 2 feet taller than the walls. Most scientists who have studied Great Zimbabwe think it was a symbol for something."

Strategy

Interact With Text by identifying the main idea and supporting details.

Write notes on your own paper to tell how you used this strategy.

"So it wasn't used for storing grain or as a lookout tower?" Tony asked.

"No," his dad said. "It may have stood for the strength of the people or the strength of the rulers. It may have been a symbol for having plenty of food. This enclosure was probably where the rulers lived. They built houses of clay with roofs made of grass and then built the walls around the houses.

The houses have mostly broken down, though. Clay doesn't last as long as stone."

Rock formation at Great Zimbabwe National Monument

[61]

Cooking the Stone

"Look, there's Mom." Tony and his dad walked over to where Tony's mom was listening to a guide.

"It is interesting how the builders **obtained** the stone," the guide was saying. "All around here are places where rocks stick up above the soil. And I mean BIG rocks. If you look up, you will see the Hill **Fortress** high above us." He **gestured** to another rock formation on a hill about half a mile away. "You'll see that the whole hill the ruins are sitting on is one piece of granite!"

Tony was impatient. "Excuse me, sir, but what does that have to do with getting the stone for the walls?"

"The builders would build a fire on top of or around a giant hunk of granite until the rock got very hot," the guide explained. "Then they poured cold, cold water on the hot rock. The change in temperature caused the rock to crack into flat slabs, almost like bricks. In a way, the Zimbabwe builders cooked the stone!"

The ruins of Great Zimbabwe overlooking the lush land of Zimbabwe, Africa

Vo·cab·u·lar·y

obtained (uhb•**taynd**)—got

fortress (**for**•tris)—a fort; a place of safety or protection

gestured (**jes**•chuhrd)— pointed

"Cool!" Tony said. "So no one had to make bricks one by one or dig rock out of the ground."

"That's right," said the guide. "But the building of the Great Enclosure, the Hill Fortress, and the many other enclosures that are gone now still took a very large amount of skill. No European cultures at that time could build such fine walls without mortar. The wall also shows that the culture was successful enough for people to take time away from meeting their daily needs for food and shelter to work on this project." The guide looked at his watch. "Take a few more minutes here and then we'll take the trail up to the Hill Fortress."

Strategy

Interact With Text by identifying the main idea and supporting details.

Write notes on your own paper to tell how you used this strategy.

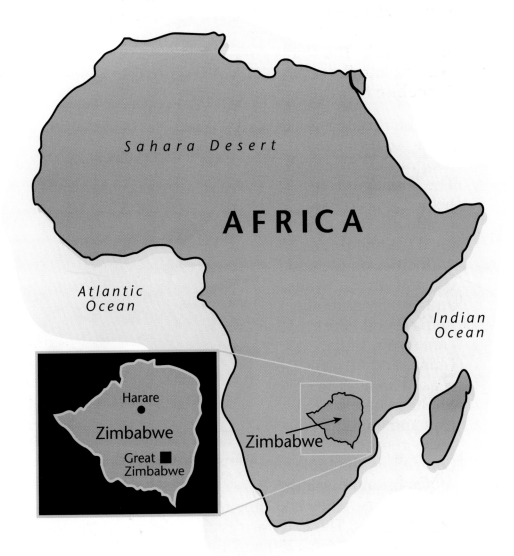

Sahara Desert

AFRICA

Atlantic
Ocean

Indian
Ocean

Harare
Zimbabwe
Great ■
Zimbabwe

Zimbabwe

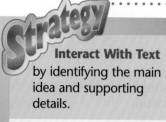

The Hill Fortress

Of course, Tony couldn't wait. He spotted the trail and reached the Hill Fortress well before the tour group. His dad was right behind him. The Hill Fortress looked different. It was older and not as even as the Great Enclosure. In many places, parts of the granite hill stuck out of the ground, and stones were fitted around the natural rock to make the wall. Tony and his dad explored three areas that looked as if they used to be walled off.

When the tour group came up, the guide was talking about the history of the African people who built Great Zimbabwe. "Early Shona [**shoh**•nuh] people settled in this area of Africa more than a thousand years ago. It's a high area, and the rainfall was good.

"The people herded cattle, so they needed the grass to grow well. The abundant rain helped this growth. Gradually, they developed trading routes with cities on the east coast of Africa. Beads and pottery and other items found here came from India, China, and African coastal areas. The Shona people traded iron and gold for these items. Controlling the trade routes brought wealth

Ruins of a stairway at Great Zimbabwe

to the people. They had time to develop government and a ruling class. The Hill Fortress and the Great Enclosure were built between 1250 and 1400."

Tony interrupted. "It's the ruling class that lived here in the fortress, right?"

"Yes," the guide answered. "The most important people probably lived up here in the fortress. Other rulers lived in the Great Enclosure. Some scientists think that the walls of the Great Enclosure were built just for show. The rulers wanted everyone to see how important they were!"

A Mystery to Solve

Tony interrupted again. "If they were so important, where are they now? What happened to the people who lived in Great Zimbabwe?"

"That, young friend, is the million-dollar question," the guide said. "By about 500 years ago, this great fortress and the enclosure in the valley below were deserted. No one really knows why this place was built, and no one knows why it was **abandoned**. No one knows what the tower was for. It's a great mystery." He smiled at Tony. "Do you like to solve mysteries?"

"I sure do," Tony answered.

"Well, then, maybe the solution of this mystery is for you!"

Vo•cab•u•lar•y

abandoned
(uh•**ban**•duhnd)—left behind

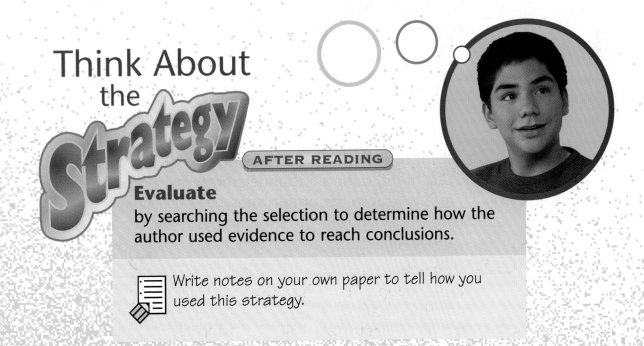

Think About the Strategy

AFTER READING

Evaluate
by searching the selection to determine how the author used evidence to reach conclusions.

Write notes on your own paper to tell how you used this strategy.

Word Roots

Many word parts in English words come from Greek and Latin. *Fort* is a **word root** from the Latin word *fortis*, meaning "strong." When you read a word that contains the root *fort*, think about how "strong" is part of the meaning of the whole word.

Read the following sentence from "The Mystery of Great Zimbabwe." It contains a word with the root *fort*:

*If you look up, you will see the Hill **Fortress** high above us.*

The root *fort* is in the word *fortress*. A *fortress* is "a strong and secure place for safety or protection."

Each of the sentences below contains an underlined word with the word root *fort*. As you read each sentence, think about the ways in which "strong" is part of the meaning of the underlined word. Then write each underlined word on a separate sheet of paper. Explain how "strong" is a part of the meaning of that word. Compare your answers with the definitions of the words in a dictionary.

1. Milk is <u>fortified</u> with vitamins A and D.
2. If math is your <u>forte</u>, help others study after school to improve their grades.
3. <u>Fortitude</u> is what helped the fourth-grade soccer team beat the fifth-grade team.
4. Last night, during a thunderstorm, my mom came into my room to <u>comfort</u> me.
5. We made a <u>fort</u> in the snow to get ready for a snowball fight.

Poetry

Read the poem as if you were Tony and you were thinking over what you had just seen. Practice reading the poem, and then present it to the class.

Fluency **TIP**

As you read and practice this poem, notice that there are five beats per line. Read with a sense of rhythm.

Walls Without Mortar

Walls without mortar,
Create shapes that glow.
A fit so perfect
The skilled builders know.

For Great Enclosures
Men carry boulders
Along many paths,
Up on their shoulders.

Light up a hot fire.
Heat sizzles on rocks.
Then comes the loud crack!
Cold rock turns to blocks.

Granite homes for kings.
Others lived around.
Rock stays long after
People can be found.

By fifteen hundred,
In Great Zimbabwe
People no longer
Did walk the highway.

Tony and his dad
Stare at Fortress Hill
That rose in the sky—
A sign of great will.

Just rocks and rubble,
This beautiful site.
It withers and wastes
In an ancient light.

"What happened?" you ask.
No one really knows.
Tony's on the case.
The mystery grows.

Now it's up to you.
Want to climb and dance
All among the rocks?
Want to take that chance?

Think About
the
Strategies

BEFORE READING

Activate Prior Knowledge
by looking at the title, headings, pictures, and graphics to decide what I know about this topic.

DURING READING

Interact With Text
by identifying the main idea and supporting details.

AFTER READING

Evaluate
by searching the selection to determine how the author used evidence to reach conclusions.

 Use your own paper to jot notes to apply these Before, During, and After Reading Strategies. In this selection, you will choose when to stop, think, and respond.

A Story of the Anasazi

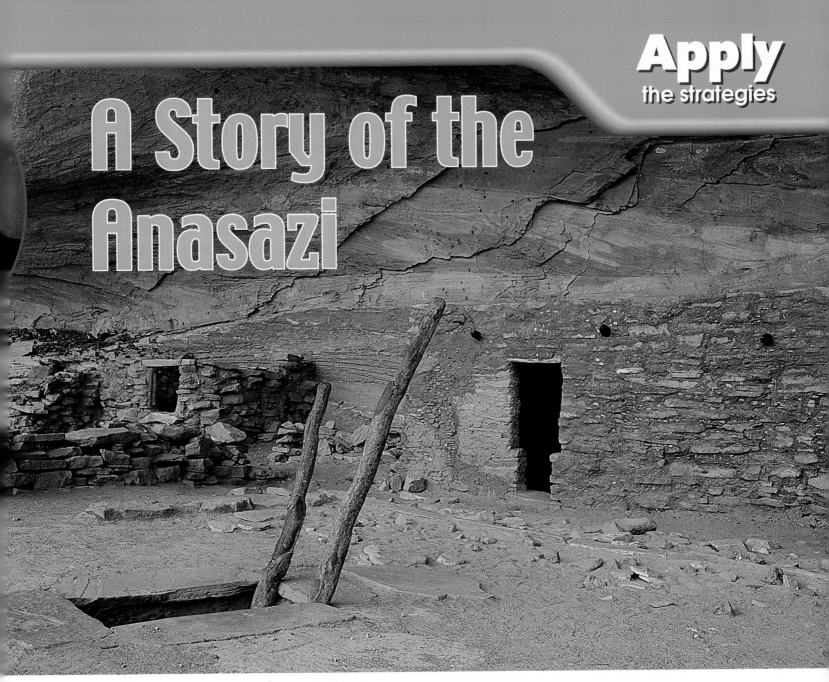

Ancient dwellings in the American Southwest

About 2,000 years ago, a group of wanderers hunted animals and gathered food plants. They lived in the area we now call the American Southwest. In one area, they noticed that there were many animals for food. And the plants grew well. These areas, called **mesas,** were high up. And they were cut by narrow canyons.

In some places, the walls of the canyons were worn away. There were huge shallow caves in the rock. The wanderers took shelter in these caves. They hunted and gathered on the mesas above. The weather was warm and dry. The people spent most of their time outdoors. These people are now known as the Anasazi [ah•nuh•**sah**•zee].

Vo•**cab**•u•lar•y

mesas (**may**•suhz)—high, flat areas of land, like tabletops

[69]

The Pit House Time

By the year 700, the people were living in houses up on the mesas. Their houses were called pit houses. These Anasazi people made a certain kind of basket. When that type of basket is found, we know that those Anasazi lived in pit houses. The **remains** of the pit houses are still there today.

A pit with a flat bottom was dug in the earth. Wooden poles held up a roof of sticks and mud. There was a hole in the center of the roof. This allowed smoke to get out. That's also how the people got in and out of the house. They put a ladder in the hole.

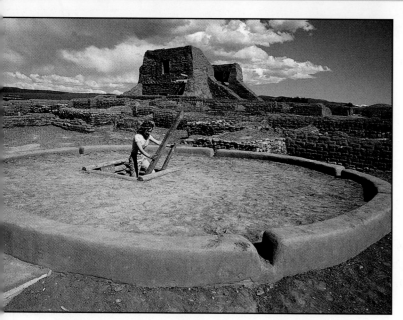

Tourist exploring a pit house ruin at Pecos National Monument, New Mexico

Scientists are able to tell how old the pit houses are. They count the growth rings in the wooden poles. But no one knows why the people moved from the caves up to the mesas.

Early Pueblos

Gradually, the Anasazi built their homes aboveground. In time, they built rows of one-room homes. These homes shared a wall. They were like a row of apartments. The buildings built this way are called **pueblos**. Families probably lived together in the same row.

In time, the people made the houses out of sandstone bricks instead of sticks and mud. By 1050, the people were living above the ground. These houses had two stories.

The Anasazi who lived in pueblos made a certain kind of pottery. When that pottery is found, we know that those Anasazi lived during the time of the pueblos. They relied on farming for much of their food.

When the people moved aboveground, two things remained from the earlier time. First, they had to go up to go down. The first-floor rooms usually didn't have a door. People climbed up a ladder to the roof. Then they went down another ladder to get inside.

Vo·cab·u·lar·y

remains (ri•**maynz**)—what is left over

pueblos (**pweb**•lohz)— villages built by certain Native American peoples in what is now southwestern United States

The second thing that stayed the same was the presence of a pit house. But now the pit house became a community center instead of a home. Religious meetings were held there.

Pit houses that served the community were called **kivas**. When the Anasazi lived as a distinct group of people, they had kivas. The kiva was round. It eventually came to be made of brick. But it was always underground. Historians and scientists can only guess at how the kivas were used. No written records exist. Every kiva had a fireplace. It also had a special hole in the ground called a **sipapu**. The sipapu stood for the place where living things had first come from the earth.

Ceremonial room, Great Kiva, Aztec Ruins National Park, New Mexico

Later Pueblos

The Anasazi built many buildings in wide Chaco [**chah**•koh] Canyon. This is in northwest New Mexico. They probably started building there about a thousand years ago. As more people came, they added more rooms and stories to the buildings. One town, called Pueblo Bonito [boh•**nee**•toh], is still there today. The town was made of one very large building. It had 800 rooms and 37 kivas!

The pueblos at Chaco Canyon are a mystery. No one knows why the Anasazi chose to build such large settlements there. Water was hard to get then and now. And the location doesn't seem to be close to any other important places. But at one time Pueblo Bonito must have been a very busy place. Imagine people climbing ladders into and out of the 800 rooms. Smoke is coming from openings in the roofs. Perhaps the sound of chanting is coming from one of the kivas.

Pueblo Bonito, Chaco Canyon, New Mexico

Vo•cab•u•lar•y

kivas (kee•vuhz)—special chambers used for ceremonies or council meetings

sipapu (si•pah•poo)—a ceremonial opening in the ground in a kiva

The Anasazi built with the sandstone that was all around them. Sandstone is a soft type of rock. It is often gold or golden brown. The Anasazi used stone and bone tools to loosen and shape their bricks. They had no metal, such as iron or copper. They held the bricks together with a thick mud mortar. They often put a layer of plaster over the surface of the bricks. This made them look smooth.

Anasazi people had busy lives. They went to distant areas to trade. They had a complex set of religious rituals. They were skilled in building, pottery, and weaving. They even built roads. Miles and miles of wide, flat roads lead out in every direction from the Chaco Canyon pueblos.

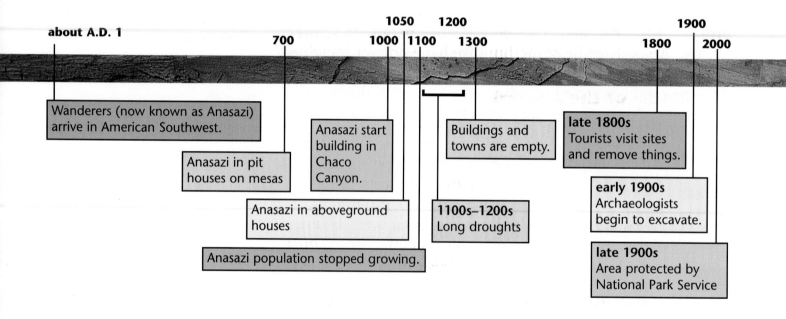

about A.D. 1   700   1000 1050 1100 1200 1300   1800 1900 2000

Wanderers (now known as Anasazi) arrive in American Southwest.

Anasazi in pit houses on mesas

Anasazi start building in Chaco Canyon.

Anasazi in aboveground houses

Anasazi population stopped growing.

Buildings and towns are empty.

1100s–1200s Long droughts

late 1800s Tourists visit sites and remove things.

early 1900s Archaeologists begin to excavate.

late 1900s Area protected by National Park Service

Back to the Cliffs

At about the same time they began building cities like Pueblo Bonito, the Anasazi began to return to the caves. No one knows why. They took their building methods with them. They carried thousands of their sandstone bricks up the faces of the cliffs. They had to use ladders and toe-holds. High up in the face of the cliff, they built huge, complex buildings in large caves.

The buildings in the cliff were just as complex as the ones they had built on the valley floor in Chaco Canyon. In some areas, wherever there is a cave of any size, there is a pueblo inside. It might be 2 rooms or it might be 50.

A pueblo called Cliff Palace is at Mesa Verde [**vair**•day] National Park. It is an example of a large cliff dwelling.

Sometime around 1100, the Anasazi population stopped growing. The people stopped building. By the year 1300, the beautiful buildings and busy towns were empty. What happened? There were lengthy droughts in the 1100s and the 1200s. These may have led people to move to wetter places. There may have been fights among the rulers of different groups of the Anasazi. This could cause people to scatter. Or the reason may be something we have not yet imagined.

Ruins of cliff dwellings, Mesa Verde National Park, Colorado

The Riddle of the Anasazi

The Anasazi people moved away to live with other groups in the area. But the buildings were preserved by the very dryness that may have led to their being deserted. They and the people who built them came to public awareness in the late 1800s. It became a popular activity to go to Anasazi places to look for old pots, baskets, and other remains of these people. Several people set up business as tour guides. They earned money for showing people where the most interesting places were.

Archaeologists first excavated Anasazi sites in the first decade of the 1900s. Now many of the important places are under the protection of the National Park Service. It makes sure that the Anasazi places are not damaged.

Many people have studied and thought about the Anasazi. They try to put the clues together. They want to solve the riddles of this ancient American culture. Still, all that can be offered is a story of the Anasazi. There are many opinions, and many arguments, about how they lived and why they died. But there are no real explanations.

The one voice missing is the voice of the Anasazi themselves. They speak only through the buildings, baskets, and pots they left behind. But listen closely. As the wind blows through the ruins, maybe we can hear their voices.

Anasazi pottery

Synonyms

Synonyms are words that have the same or similar meaning. Look at the saying "Welcome to my abode. Please make yourself at home." *Abode* and *home* are synonyms.

Writers use synonyms when they do not want to repeat a certain word. You can find synonyms in a thesaurus. A thesaurus is similar to a dictionary. It is a book of words in alphabetical order that gives both synonyms and antonyms for each word. Using synonyms can make your writing more exciting and descriptive. Synonyms used for *home* and *abode* in "A Story of the Anasazi" are *shelter* and *dwelling*.

Look at this sample entry from a thesaurus. Notice the different features included in the entry; for example, *n.* tells you that this entry word is a noun.

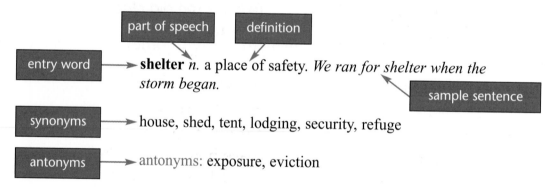

part of speech   definition

entry word → **shelter** *n.* a place of safety. *We ran for shelter when the storm began.*

sample sentence

synonyms → house, shed, tent, lodging, security, refuge

antonyms → antonyms: exposure, eviction

On a separate sheet of paper, write at least one synonym for each of these words from "A Story of the Anasazi." Use a thesaurus if you need help.

1. wanderer
2. canyon
3. houses
4. door
5. farming

6. location
7. sound
8. imagine
9. rock
10. rulers

Poetry

With a partner, read the poem and practice calling the lines back and forth to each other, from one side of the classroom to the other. Use soft and loud voices when the poem calls for them. For example, you might want to say the verses somewhat loudly and then call the refrain, "Do you hear them?" somewhat softly.

Fluency TIP

As you practice and present this poem, make your voice soft and loud at the appropriate places in the poem. Be sure to make the refrain "Do you hear them?" sound like a question.

Do You Hear Them?

The stories remain,
Calling down through time.
People's tales linger
In sandstone and lime.

Do you hear them?

Descend the ladder
To the sipapu,
Symbols of times past
From pit to Picchu.

Do you hear them?

See deep in canyons.
Look closely at cliffs.
From kivas to hills—
Hear tales that uplift.

Do you hear them?

Clues appear in rock.
Curious ladders
Lead to empty towns
And tales that matter.

Do you hear them?

Many search today
To solve the old clues.
See signs of power
In yesterday's news.

Do you hear them?

The Inca, Shona,
Anasazi, too,
Leave homes and culture
For us to sort through.

Do you hear them?

The stories remain,
Calling down through time.
People's tales linger
In sandstone and lime.

Do you hear them?

Map

This map shows Peru, in South America. Can you find Machu Picchu? Answer the questions on the next page.

Discussion Questions

Answer these questions with a partner or on a separate sheet of paper.

1. Which sentence describes Peru? Let the compass rose, or the direction finder, help you.
   a. Peru is west of Brazil.
   b. Peru is east of Brazil.
   c. Peru is almost surrounded by the Pacific Ocean.
   d. Peru is north of Ecuador.

2. Describe where Machu Picchu is on the map.

3. If you hiked west from Machu Picchu, what would you reach first?
   a. the Pacific Ocean
   b. Brazil
   c. Lima
   d. the Andes Mountains

4. You want to travel overland to reach Machu Picchu. From which place would it be easiest to reach this city?
   a. from the ocean
   b. from Ecuador
   c. from Brazil
   d. from Bolivia

5. Why would it be difficult to drive to Machu Picchu from Lima?

6. Is it appropriate for Peru to use Machu Picchu as a tourist attraction? Expain your answer.

7. Do you think all the lost cities in Peru have been found? Explain your answer.

8. Is it likely that there are lost cities in the United States?
   a. Yes, because the Spaniards invaded North America, too.
   b. Yes, because the Incas once lived in Mexico.
   c. No, because hikers or planes would have spotted the cities by now.
   d. No, because people would not desert a city in the United States.

EXPLORE MORE

Write a Travel Ad

Visit a travel agency, and ask for information and travel guides to one of the places in this unit. Use the information to write an advertisement to convince people to travel there. Be sure to give the location of the place, the best way or ways to travel there, the typical weather at certain times of the year, and any special features unique to that particular place. Add pictures or drawings to complete your advertisement.

Andean Music

Explore some Andean music. Many of the Indians living in the Andes Mountains are preserving traditional music of the area, especially music with a special flute and drums. Visit your library or a place that sells musical recordings, and find an album of some of this music. Share your favorite songs with a partner or with the whole class.

Be a Reporter

Imagine you are an investigative reporter doing a special report on one of the places and cultures presented in this unit. Describe what people might see, hear, smell, taste, and touch in that place. Include a short interview with at least one person there, identifying who the person is and what role he or she has there. Add illustrations, and present the report either orally or in written form.

A Diorama

Build a diorama to display a family's room in a pueblo or to show what a kiva may have looked like. Add specific Anasazi details, such as pottery and baskets.

A Travel Guide

Pretend to be a travel guide at the Great Zimbabwe. Write a script of what you would tell visitors about a certain part of the ruins. Do some research, and be sure to include facts about the place as it is now and historic information about the Shona people who lived there.

Solve a Mystery

Choose an ancient mystery presented in this unit. Write an explanation of what may have happened to cause the people to abandon their special place.

Related Books

Bessire, Mark. *Great Zimbabwe*. Franklin Watts, Incorporated, 1999.

Bial, Raymond. *Lifeways: The Pueblo*. Benchmark Books, 2000.

Bingham, Hiram. *The Ancient Incas: Chronicles From National Geographic*. Chelsea House Publishers,1999.

Bishop, Amanda, and Bobbie Kalman. *Life in a Pueblo*. Crabtree Publishing Company, 2003.

Larson, Timothy. *Anasazi*. Steadwell Books, 2001.

Lewin, Ted. *Lost City: The Discovery of Machu Picchu*. Philomel Books, 2003.

Mann, Elizabeth. *Machu Picchu*. Mikaya Press, 2000.

Stefoff, Rebecca. *Finding the Lost Cities*. Oxford University Press, 1997.

Interesting Web Sites

Crow Canyon Archaeological Center Use virtual field trips to explore the site of the ancient Puebloans.
http://www.crowcanyon.org/EducationProducts/ElecFieldTrip_CRP/index.html

Great Zimbabwe This is a pictorial tour of Great Zimbabwe.
http://www.cultures.com/features/Africa/zimbabwe/zimbabwe.html

Machu Picchu Information and photographs give a good overview of this place.
http://www.mnsu.edu/emuseum/prehistory/latinamerica/south/sites/machu_picchu.html

Machu Picchu, Peru Beautiful photographs show a few of the important and interesting places in Machu Picchu.
http://www.sacredsites.com/2nd56/21422.html

Mystery of Great Zimbabwe Here are photographs and information about this ancient place in Africa.
http://www.pbs.org/wgbh/nova/israel/zimbabwe.html

Sipapu—The Anasazi Emergence into the Cyber World This site gives information on the history and architecture of the Anasazi. It includes 3D models and videos.
http://sipapu.gsu.edu/

Web sites have been carefully researched for accuracy, content, and appropriateness. However, teachers and caregivers are reminded that Web sites are subject to change. Internet use should always be monitored.

Unit 3
Strategies

BEFORE READING

Set a Purpose

by using the title and headings to write questions that I can answer while I am reading.

DURING READING

Clarify Understanding

by using photographs, charts, and other graphics to help me understand what I'm reading.

AFTER READING

Respond

by drawing logical conclusions about the topic.

LEARN
the **strategies**
in the selection
A Love for Lacrosse
page 83

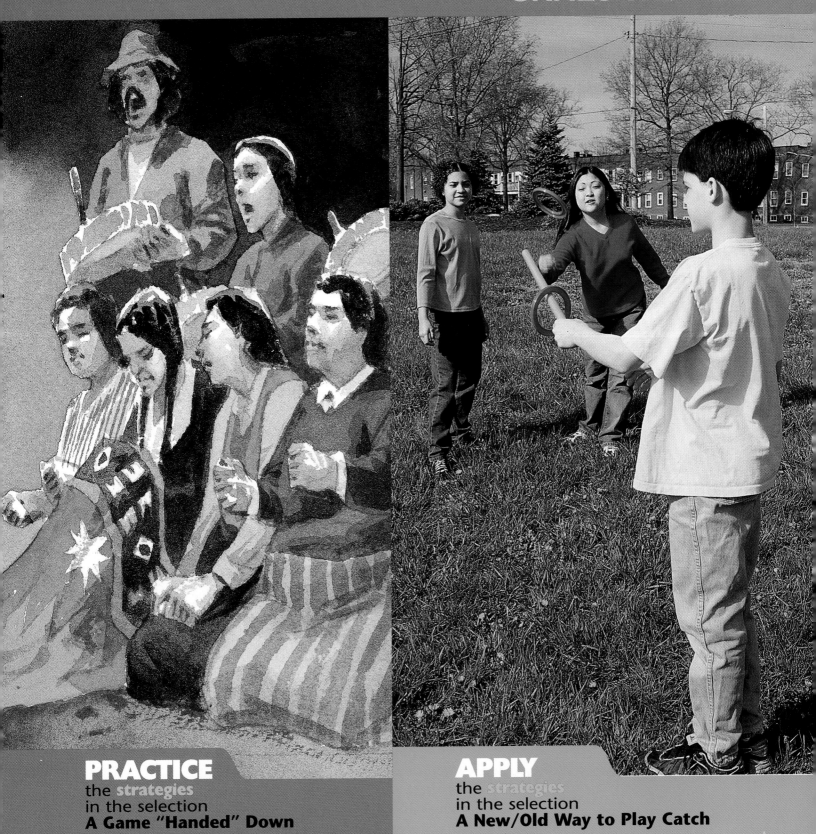

PRACTICE
the strategies
in the selection
A Game "Handed" Down
page 95

APPLY
the strategies
in the selection
A New/Old Way to Play Catch
page 105

Think About the Strategies

Set a Purpose

by using the title and headings to write questions that I can answer while I am reading.

My Thinking

The strategy says to use the title and headings to write questions that I can answer while I am reading. The title is "A Love for Lacrosse." My first question is "What is lacrosse?" The first heading is "The First Lacrosse Games." My question is "What is some of the history of lacrosse?" The next heading is "Tamer Times." I want to know what this heading means, so I'll have to read to find out. The heading "Looking Back" makes me want to know what I will be looking back at. The last heading is "Traditions Continue." My question is "What are the traditions?" I'll look for the answers to my questions while I am reading.

Clarify Understanding

by using photographs, charts, and other graphics to help me understand what I'm reading.

My Thinking

The strategy says to clarify understanding by using photographs, charts, and other graphics to help me understand what I'm reading. I will stop and think about this strategy every time I come to a red button like this ●.

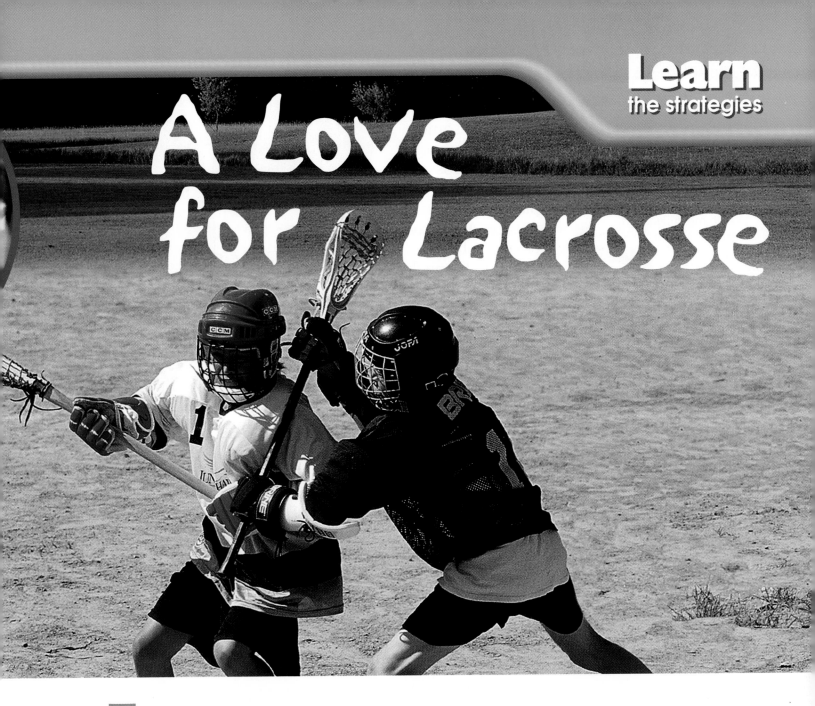

The game of lacrosse was given its name by a French **missionary**. However, the game was invented by Native Americans. Members of the Iroquois nation developed the **version** of lacrosse that is now played. Choctaw men also played—and still play—another version of the game. There is great enthusiasm for lacrosse.

Europeans were still new to North America. French settlers watched Native American teams play this game. The settlers put together their own teams. They wanted to play each other. By 1867, lacrosse had become the national sport of Canada. Now it's played throughout the world.

Vo•cab•u•lar•y

missionary (**mish**•uh•ner•ee)—a person sent to another culture to introduce his or her religion to the native people of that culture

version (**vur**•zhuhn)—one of various ways of doing something

[83]

Clarify Understanding
by using photographs, charts, and other graphics to help me understand what I'm reading.

My Thinking
The photograph on this page shows a man making lacrosse sticks. I know he's working with wood because I can see the wood shavings on the floor. But I still don't know for sure what his shaped wood will look like. I'll keep reading.

Lacrosse is similar in some ways to ice hockey. But lacrosse is different, too. It is played on grass, not ice. And players use a ball instead of a puck. Lacrosse sticks are even shaped differently. Their shape allows players to scoop up the ball and throw it.

Making lacrosse sticks is an art form.

The First Lacrosse Games

Native Americans played lacrosse long ago. The ball they used was made of stuffed deerskin. Like modern sticks, their sticks had a hoop at one end. Leather strips **crisscrossed** the hoop. The strips formed a pocket. Players could catch or scoop up and throw the ball. The hoops used by different Native American groups were shaped slightly differently. Some groups used two sticks, one in each hand. Others used one stick.

To that French missionary long ago, the stick looked like a **bishop**'s cross, so he called the game "lacrosse." Two Native American names for the game are *tokonhon* [tah•**kohn**•huhn] and *ishtaboli* [ish•tah•**boh**•lee]. Both names mean "little-brother-of-war." For Native Americans, one purpose of the game was to test the strength and courage of young **warriors**.

In games long ago, the playing field might be a different size for every game. Sometimes the field stretched for a mile across the meadow or prairie. Teams could have any number of players. But both sides were even. There might be hundreds of players spread across the field battling each other. They were trying to send the ball between their

Vo • cab • u • lar • y

crisscrossed (kris•krawst)—
went back and forth across each other

bishop (bish•uhp)—a high-ranking member of a church

warriors (wor•ee•uhrz)—
people who fight in wars

opponents' goal posts at the end of the field. In the 1830s, the artist George Catlin painted one of these large groups of players struggling with each other.

A game might last for days. During that time, players might be stomped, trampled, tackled, and kicked. Some of them were badly injured and even killed!

"Ball Play of the Choctaw—Ball Up" painted by George Catlin

Tamer Times

Today, men's lacrosse is played on a field that measures 60 by 110 yards. The field for women's lacrosse is usually 70 by 120 yards. At each end are goals. They look much like hockey nets. The ball is made of hard rubber. It is a little smaller than a tennis ball.

Each player carries one stick, or crosse. The end of the stick splits apart. This forms an opening. The opening is filled with a net of leather strips or strong cord. The **goalie** carries a crosse with a wider net.

Men's teams have 10 players. Women's teams have 12. The object is to use the crosse to pass the ball. It goes from one team member to another until it is sent into the **opposing** team's goal. Players are not allowed to touch the ball with their hands.

Vo·cab·u·lar·y

opponents
(uh•**poh**•nuhnts)—people who work or fight against each other

goalie (**goh**•lee)—
the goalkeeper, or player who protects the goal so opponents can't score

opposing (uh•**poh**•zing)—on the other side

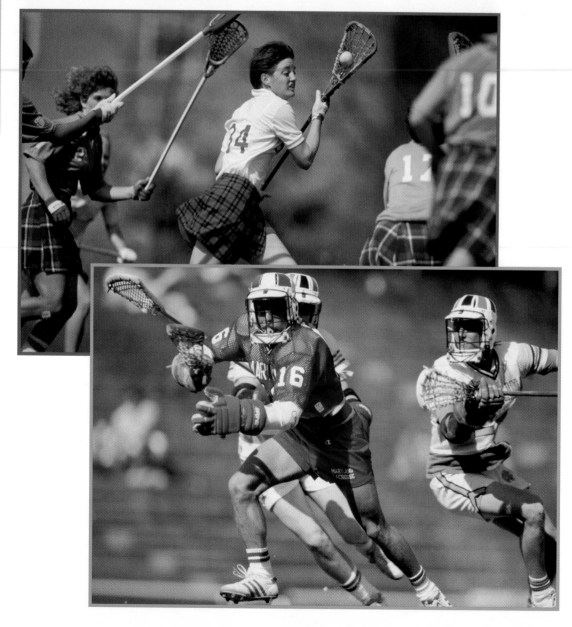

The game is played for an hour. The time is divided into four periods. Players wear special gear to prevent injuries. They may wear helmets with face guards, shoulder and arm padding, and gloves. Their uniforms are similar to those worn by ice hockey players.

Box lacrosse is played in a smaller, enclosed area. Often it's played indoors. Teams have only six players. And there's lots of body contact. Box lacrosse is popular in Canada and the United States. And there are many Iroquois teams.

Men's and women's lacrosse teams

Iroquois National vs. Oneonta State College

Strategy

Clarify Understanding by using photographs, charts, and other graphics to help me understand what I'm reading.

My Thinking
One of the players in this photograph is on an Iroquois team. This goes along with what the selection is saying, so that makes sense. The Iroquois still like to play lacrosse.

Looking Back

Lacrosse is an important part of the Iroquois tradition. Long ago, it was played for fun. It also helped to settle disputes among groups. The Iroquois believed that playing lacrosse would help heal the sick. The game could lift people's hearts. The game also prepared young men for battle. And it helped older warriors stay in shape.

In the 1800s, Native American lacrosse teams were banned from competing in **amateur** national or international games. Some of these teams had charged admission to their games. This was against the rules for amateur teams. But they had been trying to raise money so they could travel to other games.

In 1987, the Iroquois National team was formed. Native American teams were finally allowed to play in amateur competitions. Since then, the Iroquois team has challenged other teams in the World Games and other international competitions.

Vo•cab•u•lar•y

amateur (am•uh•tur)— involving players who do not get paid for what they do

[87]

Clarify Understanding by using photographs, charts, and other graphics to help me understand what I'm reading.

My Thinking
This chart shows the Iroquois team in second place. It looks like the Iroquois still take their lacrosse seriously. I wonder what the standings are now.

World Indoor Lacrosse Championship 2003 Division Standings		
Team	Won	Lost
1. Canada	5	0
2. Iroquois	4	1
3. Scotland	3	2
4. United States	2	3
5. Australia	1	4
6. Czech Republic	0	5

Only Canada's team had a better record than the Iroquois in the 2003 standings.

Traditions Continue

At Iroquois cultural celebrations today, people can watch the dances and taste the food. And they can buy

A tradition that spans generations

handmade items, including lacrosse sticks. Many of these events include a series of lacrosse games. Whether the Iroquois still live in the homes of their ancestors or in big cities, the game of lacrosse brings them together. It's a link to their past. And it's an important part of their present.

Think About the Strategy

AFTER READING

Respond
by drawing logical conclusions about the topic.

My Thinking
The strategy says I should respond by drawing logical conclusions about the topic. I think that means to come to conclusions that make sense. Well, the information in the first parts of the selection makes me conclude that the Native Americans had at least some free time. They liked to have fun and to play games. They didn't have computers and televisions and things like that, so they made up their own games. Lacrosse has been around for a long time. There are a lot of lacrosse teams now, so the game is popular with a lot of people. Native American teams show that they still like the game.

Graphic organizers help us organize information we read. I think this text can be organized by using a comparison matrix. Here is how I organized the information. I decided to compare early and modern lacrosse games. In the first column, I listed three main parts of the game. Under the two headings, I added facts and information.

Comparison Matrix
A Love for Lacrosse

	Early Lacrosse Games	Modern Lacrosse Games
equipment	• ball made of stuffed deerskin • sticks had hoop crisscrossed with leather • some groups, 2 sticks others, 1 stick	• ball made of hard rubber • end of stick is split, opening filled with a net of leather strips or strong cord • each player, only 1 stick • helmets with face guards, shoulder and arm padding, and gloves
playing field	• could be a different size for every game • could stretch for a mile • goal posts at each end	• men's field, 60 by 110 yards • women's field, 70 by 120 yards • goal at each end much like a hockey net
teams	• could have any number of players, with both sides even • could last for days • hardly any rules	• men's teams, 10 players • women's teams, 12 players • game time—1 hour • box lacrosse—a lot of body contact

I used my graphic organizer to write a summary of the article. Can you find the information in my summary that came from my comparison matrix?

A Summary of
A Love for Lacrosse

Native Americans invented the game of lacrosse, and Native Americans still play it. The modern game is the same as the early game in some ways and different in other ways. I am going to compare the equipment, the playing field, and the teams from the past and the present.

Long ago, the ball was made of stuffed deerskin. The sticks ended in a hoop made of leather strips. Some teams used 2 sticks, but others used 1 stick. Today, the ball is made of hard rubber. The end of the stick is split, and the opening is filled with a net of leather strips or strong cord. Each player uses only 1 stick. Today's players are safer because they may wear helmets with face guards, shoulder and arm padding, and gloves.

Long ago, the playing field might be a different size for every game. Some fields stretched for a mile. At each end was a pair of goal posts. Today, the men's field is 60 by 110 yards. The women's field is 70 by 120 yards. The field still has a goal at each end, but now it looks much like a hockey net.

Long ago, teams could have any number of players, but both sides were even. A game could last for days and had hardly any rules. Today, the men's teams have 10 players, and the women's teams have 12. Games last 1 hour. Players may have a lot of body contact, but they must follow strict rules to avoid injuries.

Lacrosse is still played as it was long ago. The safety of the players gets a lot more attention now. And today's players enjoy the game just as much as early players did!

Introduction
Here is how I developed my introductory paragraph. It gives readers an idea of what they are about to read.

Body
I wrote one paragraph each about equipment, the playing field, and teams. I used the information from my comparison matrix.

Conclusion
I summarized my paper by recalling the main ideas.

Latin Roots

Some English words have similar sounds, spellings, and meanings. This is because they come from the same Latin word. For example, the words *opponent, opposing, opposition,* and *opposite* all come from the Latin verb *opponere,* which means "to set or place against."

Read this passage from "A Love for Lacrosse." Think about how the *opponents* are "set against each other."

> *There might be hundreds of players spread across the field battling each other. They were trying to send the ball between their **opponents'** goal posts at the end of the field.*

The lacrosse players are "placed against" each other. The context of a game suggests that the word *opponents* means "people who fight or compete against each other."

Look at another passage from the selection:

> *The object is to use the crosse to pass the ball. It goes from one team member to another until it is sent into the **opposing** team's goal.*

The teams are "set against" each other. The context of a game with two teams suggests that *opposing* means "on the other side or team."

The boldface words below all come from the Latin word *opponere.* Read the sentences and think about how the definition "to set or place against" relates to the meaning of the boldface words. Write the definitions of the boldface words on a separate sheet of paper. Use a dictionary to check your work.

1. The principal was **opposed** to the idea that girls should be allowed to play football.
2. The Flintville Falcons proved to be tough **opponents,** but we won the game by one point.
3. I sat **opposite** Iggie at lunch today.
4. The **opposition** to the new playground is worried that there is not enough money to pay for it.
5. My thumb is **opposable** to my fingers.

Journal Entry

Early explorers and settlers were surprised when they saw Native Americans playing lacrosse. Luis is writing about seeing a new sport for the first time. Practice reading this imaginary journal entry several times until you are ready to perform it for the class.

Try reading this journal entry with the kind of wonder and excitement Luis must have felt as he saw lacrosse being played for the first time. Try to use a tone of voice that sounds the way you think the character might talk.

Journal of Luis Leroy, French Settler

July 14, 17—

It has been a month since we arrived in the New World. There have been so many new things to see and hear and taste! This morning I went exploring on the other side of the nearest ridge. Suddenly I came upon an enormous meadow. I saw hundreds of people holding sticks! At first I mistook them for an army. But soon I realized that the people were simply playing a sport! I sat quietly in view of the game for some time. I found it to be very exciting.

Each stick has a hoop made from leather strips at one end. The players use these sticks to throw and catch a leather ball. They try to throw the ball into the net at either end of the meadow. The game went on for a long while.

As the sun began to set, the players dispersed. But the game did not appear to be over. Perhaps I will return tomorrow and see which team will win!

Think About
the
Strategies

BEFORE READING

Set a Purpose
by using the title and headings to write questions that I can answer while I am reading.

 Write notes on your own paper to tell how you used this strategy.

DURING READING

Clarify Understanding
by using photographs, charts, and other graphics to help me understand what I'm reading.

 When you come to a red button like this ⬤, write notes on your own paper to tell how you used this strategy.

A Game "Handed" Down

Different versions of the hand game have been popular for generations.

You have probably played the hand game without knowing who invented it. It's a guessing game. One player holds an object hidden in each hand. One of the objects has a special mark on it. Another player guesses which hand has the marked object.

Does that game sound familiar? The Spanish name for the hand game is *peón* [pay•**ohn**]. Native American names include *churchúrki* [choor•**choor**•kee] and *tinsok* [**tin**•sahk].

The hand game was probably first played by the Plains Indians. However, 81 different Native American groups have played this game. Most of them lived in the western two thirds of North America. In fact, many of these groups still have hand game teams that play each other at tournaments. The hand game was and is a fun way for groups of players to try to outsmart each other. Groups can compete even if they speak different languages. They communicate with **gestures**.

The Rules of the Game

Two people can play the hand game. It can also be played by two teams with the same number of players. When teams play, the players stand or sit in rows about six feet apart. Players from each side take turns hiding the marked object and guessing its location. Long ago, the objects were often small animal bones, one plain and one painted. Some pairs of bones were hollow, while some

Vo•cab•u•lar•y

gestures (**jes•**chuhrz)—hand movements that communicate meaning

 Most children enjoy playing variations of the hand game.

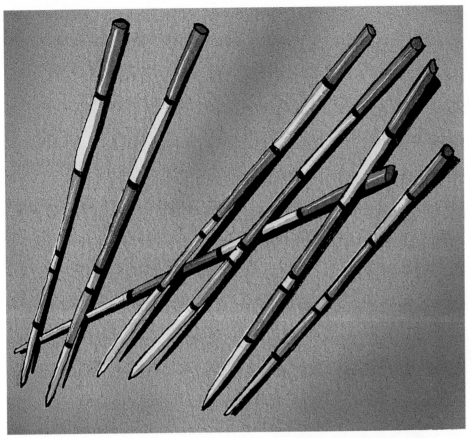

Sometimes sets of counting sticks were handed down through families.

Strategy

Clarify Understanding by using photographs, charts, and other graphics to help me understand what I'm reading.

Write notes on your own paper to tell how you used this strategy.

were solid. Sometimes one bone was marked by tying a leather strip around it. These bones were considered good luck for whoever owned them. They were passed from one **generation** to the next.

If a player correctly guesses the location of the marked object, the person or team gets a wooden counting stick. Anyone making an incorrect guess loses a stick. When one player wins all the sticks, the game ends. The winner may get a prize. Sometimes an **umpire** makes sure everyone plays fairly.

Some sets of counting sticks are elaborately carved or painted. Some of them are sharpened to a point on one end, so they can be stuck into the ground between the two teams or players. Long ago, each stick sometimes represented a horse. Players won and lost horses as they played.

Vo·cab·u·lar·y

generation (jen•uh•**ray**•shuhn)—each part of a family, such as all the brothers and sisters or all the grandparents

umpire (**um**•pyr)— a person who makes sure games are played fairly

The Tricks of the Game

During the game, the player hiding the object often makes many hand movements to confuse the guesser. For example, one player might hold his hands above his head or behind his back. Another player might hide her hand movements under a blanket on her lap. The player or team usually sings while hiding the object, and someone plays a drum. The fast beat of the drum makes the game more exciting and helps confuse the guesser.

In some Native American groups long ago, only men were allowed to play the hand game. The women cheered them on and sang. In other groups, teams of women could play each other. Today women and men both play, but the drummer is usually still a man.

People watching these games often place bets on who is going to win. A game might last all day and all night. A winning team might become not only famous but also rich.

Today, teams have colors, jackets, songs, and many supporters. Every year, 31 tribal colleges and universities meet to hold different kinds of competitions. You can be sure they play the hand game.

Singing and drumming could be the entertainment—or they could be just the distraction needed to fool an opponent!

Try Your Hand!

You and a friend can play the hand game. First, you must find two objects the same size, small enough to be hidden in your hand. Mark one of them. For example, you might gather two stones and use a marker to put a red spot on one of them. Make sure the objects are the same size. If one object is bigger than the other, the guesser will be able to tell which fist holds it.

Hand Game for Two Players

The first player will pick up the two objects and put both hands behind his or her back. When this player shows his or her hands again, the guesser must point to the hand with the marked object. If the guesser is correct, he or she gets a point. Players take turns hiding the objects and guessing the location of the marked one.

Strategy

Clarify Understanding by using photographs, charts, and other graphics to help me understand what I'm reading.

Write notes on your own paper to tell how you used this strategy.

The hand game is good for teams and for just two players.

All you need to begin are two small objects—one plain and one marked.

Clarify Understanding by using photographs, charts, and other graphics to help me understand what I'm reading.

 Write notes on your own paper to tell how you used this strategy.

Hand Game for Teams

The teams sit facing each other. Both teams should have the same number of players. The teams can play the same way as described previously, with members of each team taking turns hiding and guessing.

In another version, the teams can play this way: The first player on one team will hide both objects in his or her hands. Then this player will pass one object to the next player on his or her team. The opposing team must guess whether the first player passed the marked object or kept it. If the team guesses correctly, it gets both objects and earns a point. Then the first player on the other team hides the objects and passes one on to a teammate.

Tillikum

Native Americans in the Northwest played this hand game. *Tillikum* means "friend" in the Chinook language. Two players or two teams can play. These are the hand signals for playing tillikum:

> **Earth** = right hand held out with palm facing down (as flat land)
> **Water** = right hand held out with fingers and thumb hanging down (as falling water)
> **Fire** = palm of right hand facing forward, with fingers and thumb pointing up (as flames of a fire)

Partners or teams stand facing each other, their right hands in fists. Someone says, "Go!" and the players raise their right fists to shoulder height three times, all together. Players can call "One, two, three" or "Til, li, kum." On "three" or "kum," players open their fists to make an Earth, Water, or Fire signal. This is how the scoring is done:

> Earth drinks Water; Earth wins.
> Water puts out Fire; Water wins.
> Fire scorches Earth; Fire wins.

If teams are playing, each team leader must tell team members which hand signals to use before play begins. If players tie, the turn is played again. The first to win three rounds wins the game.

If someone asks how you learned this game, say, "Native Americans taught me!"

You and your friends might enjoy thinking up your own versions of the hand game!

Think About the Strategy

AFTER READING

Respond

by drawing logical conclusions about the topic.

Write notes on your own paper to tell how you used this strategy.

Vocabulary

Sports Words

Some words are used mostly in a certain context. For instance, the words *inning, bunt,* and *shortstop* are all words related to baseball. To understand specialized vocabulary words, identify the overall subject that you are reading about. Then use the clues in that sentence and in the surrounding sentences to help you find the meaning of the special word.

In "A Game 'Handed' Down," the writer uses the word *umpire*:

> Sometimes an **umpire** makes sure everyone plays fairly.

The subject of the passage is a game or sport. The context clues in the sentence are the words *plays* and *fairly*. The context clues suggest that an *umpire* is similar to a judge. A judge watches that the rules of the law are followed in a courtroom. An *umpire* is a judge of a sport or a game. An *umpire* watches and makes sure the rules of the game are followed.

Read the following sentences and find the meaning of the boldface words. Look for context clues to help you. Write your answers on a separate sheet of paper. Then check your answers with the definitions in a dictionary.

1. My brother is a much better tennis player than I am. I can't win a single point. The score is always
   me: **love**
   my brother: six.

2. As the **pitcher** of a baseball team, you have to throw the ball with speed and accuracy.

3. To score a **touchdown** in football, a player must have possession of the ball in the opponent's end zone.

4. Ice hockey players use their hockey sticks to hit the little round **puck** with great force.

5. I like playing the **wing** position in soccer. The wing gets to run up and down the side of the field.

Poem-Song

Native American children and adults have enjoyed playing hand games for a very long time. Read this poem-song about a hand game several times to yourself. Then read the poem-song with a group. You may even want to sing it in a round!

TIP

Song melodies can help us remember things better. After reading the words to the poem, try singing the words to the tune of "Take Me Out to the Ball Game." Which sounds better? Which way is easier to read?

Let Me Teach You the Hand Game

Let me teach
You the hand game.
Let me show
You the fun.
It's been around
For a long, long time.
Play with a stone,
Or a stick, or a dime.

So just guess, guess, guess
Which hand has it.
A good guess
Could win you fame.
Choose the marked thing
And then you win
At the old hand game!

Think About the Strategies

BEFORE READING

Set a Purpose

by using the title and headings to write questions that I can answer while I am reading.

DURING READING

Clarify Understanding

by using photographs, charts, and other graphics to help me understand what I'm reading.

AFTER READING

Respond

by drawing logical conclusions about the topic.

 Use your own paper to jot notes to apply these Before, During, and After Reading Strategies. In this selection, you will choose when to stop, think, and respond.

A New/Old Way to Play Catch

These children are playing a game of "ring and pin."

Have you ever tossed up a ring and tried to catch it on a stick? If you have, then you were playing a game invented long ago by Native Americans. They played many variations of this game. Together, these are called "toss and catch" or "ring and pin" games. Native Americans played these games for fun and for prizes.

Game Pieces From Nature

The pin was a thin, pointed piece of bone, antler, or wood. It might be three to six inches long. Some Native American groups eventually traded with the European settlers for iron needles, which they used in this game.

Mastering ring and pin games requires patience and skill.

For the ring, players used whatever materials were available. For example, groups that lived on the Plains often used rings of dried buffalo skin. Groups in the Northwest used hollow deer-toe bones or salmon bones. Groups in the Southwest used dried squash **rinds**. People in the Northeast and Southeast wove rings of moose hair or grass. Instead of a ring, the Cree and other groups used a flat piece of leather with as many as 23 holes punched through it.

Vo·cab·u·lar·y

rinds (ryndz)—the skins of vegetables or fruits

The pin was connected to the ring by a strong cord. The cord was just long enough to allow the tip of the pin to enter the ring. The player held the pin in one hand and swung the ring into the air. Then he or she tried to **spear** the ring with the pin before it fell. Sometimes leather, fur, or beads were attached to the ring to give it more weight. This extra weight pulled the ring down faster and made the game more difficult.

In some games, the string of bones ended with a piece of leather. Both the bones and the leather were **pierced** with holes.

Ring Rules

Everyone—men and women, boys and girls—played ring and pin games. One person could play alone to test his or her **coordination**. Often, two players competed with each other. One player continued to toss and catch the ring until he or she missed. Then the other player took a turn. The more rings a player was able to catch, the more points he or she won. Different groups scored the bones differently. Some gave more points for bones that were closer to the pin. Some gave more points for bones that were farther from the pin.

Sticking the pin through a hole in the side of a bone might be worth 5 points. Sticking the pin lengthwise through the same bone, which is more difficult, might be worth 25 points. Sticking the pin lengthwise through 2 bones might earn 50 points. Holes in different places on a leather target were usually worth different numbers of points. A game could continue until 1 player earned 100 points—or as many as 2,000 points.

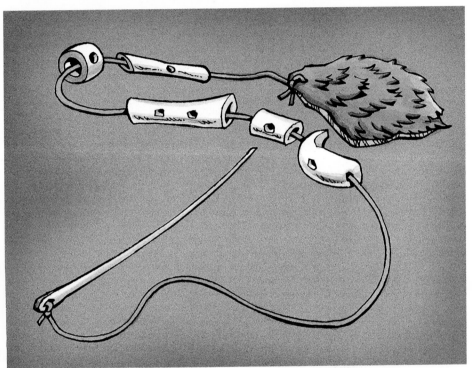

Often, the pieces of bone were allowed to slide on the cord, like these do. This sliding increased the difficulty of playing the game.

Vo·cab·u·lar·y

spear (speer)—to strike with something pointed, like a knife

pierced (peerst)—punctured

coordination (koh•or•dn•**ay**•shuhn)— the ability to use one's body well to play games or do physical work

Players often kept score by passing sticks back and forth. Each player might start out with 50 sticks, for example. When a player won points, he or she took sticks from the other player. When one player had won all the sticks, the game ended.

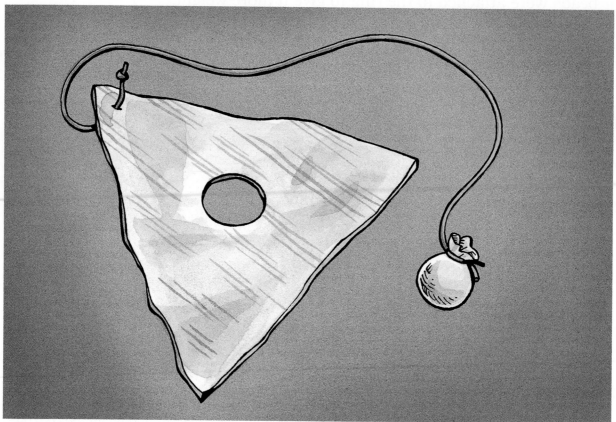

This simple equipment is used to play the ball and triangle game.

Try It Yourself

You can make a variation of this game and play it alone or with a friend. Children of the Penobscot (puh•**nob**•skuht], who lived in Maine, often played a ball and triangle game. They made their triangles out of birch bark, but you can use a piece of heavy cardboard. You will also need a small rubber ball, a seven-inch piece of string, scissors, a ruler, and tape. Directions are shown on page 109.

Making Connections

The next time you are in a toy store, look for toys that are based on the "ring and pin" or the "toss and catch" game. See if any of the games say Native Americans first played them.

Make a Ball and Triangle Game

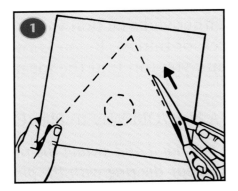

Cut a triangle out of the cardboard. Each side should be 6" long.

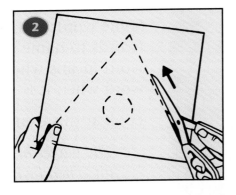

Carefully cut a hole in the center of the triangle. Make it a little bigger than the ball.

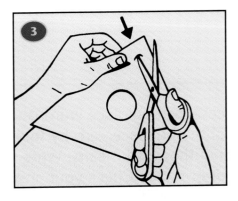

Use the scissors to punch a small hole in one corner of the triangle.

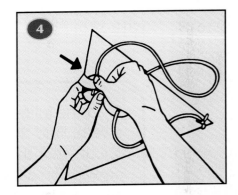

Tie one end of the string to the small hole. Firmly tape the other end of the string to the ball.

To play, hold the triangle by one of the corners without the string. Swing the ball up and try to make it fall through the hole.

Vocabulary

Parts of Speech and Meaning

Some words can be used as either verbs (action words) or as nouns (words to name people, places, or things). If you know what the word means when it is a noun, you can find the meaning of the word when it is a verb.

Look at this example from "A New/Old Way to Play Catch":

*The player held the pin in one hand and swung the ring into the air. Then he or she tried to **spear** the ring with the pin before it fell.*

You may not be familiar with the verb *spear*. But maybe you have heard of a weapon called a spear. The noun *spear* is "a weapon with a long handle and a pointed head." This knowledge can help you understand *spear* when it is used as a verb. It means "to stab with something sharp."

Read the following sentences. Each boldface word is used as a verb. Find the meaning of the boldface verb by thinking about what the noun form of the word means. Write your answers on a separate sheet of paper. Check your answers in a dictionary.

1. Juan **glued** the wings on the model airplane.
2. Since I was standing in back of the last row, I had to **crane** my neck to see the performance.
3. We **anchored** the kite to the park bench while we ate ice cream.
4. The book **mirrored** my parents' experience immigrating to the United States.
5. During the fire drill, students **streamed** down the stairwell.

Poetry

Native Americans have given us a variety of games that are fun to play. Read this poem out loud several times. When you are familiar with the lines and the rhythm, perform the poem aloud with a partner or a small group.

 **Fluency TIP**

The rhythm of the first two lines and the last two lines is the same. Remember to make your voice go up at the end of a question.

Great Games

Read about the games below.
Are they alike? Do you know?

To play lacrosse, make two teams;
Give everyone a stick.
Pass the ball to make a goal—
The players must be quick!

The hand game is a pastime
That's lots of fun to play.
Hide an object in your hand
While players "guess away."

Want to play a game of catch?
You might like "ring and pin."
Throw the ring into the air,
Catch it and you win.

Since Native Americans liked to play,
We have these great games today.

Diagram

The Basics of Men's Lacrosse

The diagram below shows the lacrosse field and the positions for one team. Here are the players and their responsibilities:

Goalie—one player protects the goal; stops the other team from scoring

Defense—three players defend their team's goal; stay in the defensive end of the field

Midfield—three players cover the entire field; play offense and defense

Attack—three players score goals; stay in the other team's end of the field

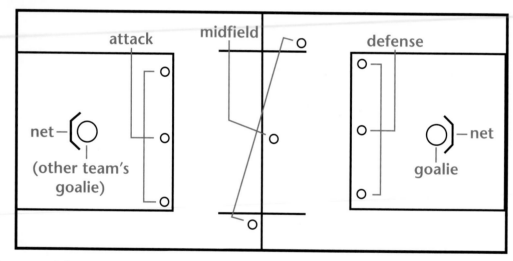

How to Play

Each quarter begins with a face-off in the center of the field. The ball is placed between a midfield player from each team. When the official blows his whistle, these two players start fighting for control of the ball. Then the other two midfield players for both teams can leave their positions. They join in the battle for control.

The attack and defense players have to wait until a player from either team gains control of the ball. Then they can leave their positions. However, the three attack players must stay on the other team's end of the field. The three defense players and the goalie must stay on their own end of the field. The three midfield players for both teams can move over the entire field. This rule prevents all twenty players from piling up on one end of the field.

The team controlling the ball tries to get it into the other team's net. Players can run with the ball, pass it, and catch it. Only the goalie can touch the ball with his hands. A goal scores one point. Then the teams take their positions again. It's time for another face-off.

Discussion Questions

Answer these questions with a partner or on a separate sheet of paper.

1. Which players can travel up and down the field?

   a. goalies
   b. defense players
   c. midfield players
   d. attack players

2. Why is the start of the game called a face-off?

3. How many players from both teams can be in one end of the field at the same time?

4. What must happen before the attack and defense players can leave their positions?

   a. The official must blow his whistle.
   b. Two midfield players must start battling for control of the ball.
   c. One team must score a goal.
   d. A player from one team must gain control of the ball.

5. How is this game like football?

   a. Both games involve 2 teams of 11 players.
   b. In both games, the teams score goals.
   c. In both games, the players use sticks to pass the ball.
   d. In both games, only the goalie can touch the ball with his hands.

6. How would this game change if all the players were allowed to touch the ball with their hands?

   a. It would be more like soccer.
   b. It would be more like football.
   c. It would be more like baseball.
   d. It would be more like volleyball.

7. Lacrosse has strict rules about body contact. Why is that?

8. Was lacrosse good training for warriors long ago? Explain your answer.

CONNECTING
to the Real World

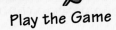

EXPLORE MORE

Games From Long Ago

Research to find another game that was popular among Native American groups long ago. Learn how to play it, and then (with a partner or a small group, if needed) explain and demonstrate the game for the class.

Be a Sportscaster

Imagine being a radio sports announcer at a Native American lacrosse game 200 years ago. Write a script that includes information about the teams and any star players, play-by-play action of several exciting parts of the game, and game strategies the players may have used. Deliver the sportscast as an oral report, or play it from an audiocassette tape.

Play the Game

With a small group, demonstrate different versions of the hand game. Then carry out a demonstration of a hand game team competition. Choose one group member to be the announcer, who can explain various rules and strategies as the play progresses.

Old/New Toys

Research on the Web, at a local toy store, or in catalogs to find modern toys similar to the ones used by Native American children in the past. Prepare a display with photographs or drawings of the toys. Write a short explanation of how each toy works.

Make a Visit

Visit a Native American Indian center in your area. You can look in your telephone directory to locate one. Contact the center to learn when a Native American cultural celebration, festival, or pow-wow is scheduled near where you live. Ask what activities are planned and if any hand game competitions are scheduled. If possible, visit the center or a pow-wow and report back to the class about your experience.

Your Own Game

Make up a hand game of your own. Decide what the goal of the game is, and set up the rules and strategies for play. Include game parts, if needed. Work with a partner or a small group, and play the game for the class.

Related Books

Bruchac, James, and Joseph Bruchac. *Native American Games and Stories*. Fulcrum Publishing, 2000.

Englar, Mary. *The Pueblo: Southwestern Potters*. Blue Earth Books, 2003.

Fletcher, Alice C. *Indian Games and Dances With Native Songs*. University of Nebraska Press, 1994.

Gendar, Jeannine. *Grass Games and Moon Races: California Indian Games and Toys*. Heyday Books, 1995.

Hegedus, Alannah, and Kaitlin Rainey. *Shooting Hoops and Skating Loops: Great Inventions in Sports*. Tundra Books, 1999.

Hoyt-Goldsmith, Diane. *Lacrosse: The National Game of the Iroquois*. Holiday House, Inc., 1998.

Hudson, Travis, and Jan Timbrook. *Chumash Indian Games*. Santa Barbara Museum of Natural History, 1997.

Macfarlan, Allan A. *Living Like Indians: A Treasury of North American Indian Crafts, Games and Activities*. Dover Publications, Inc., 1999.

Miller, Jay. *American Indian Games*. Children's Press, 1996.

Interesting Web Sites

Check out these sites to learn more about Native American arts, sports, games, and technology.

www.hickoksports.com/history/lacrosse.shtml
www.germantown.k12.il.us/html/intro.html
www.nativetech.org
www.lacrosse.org/museum/history.phtml
www.e-lacrosse.com/laxhist.htm
www.americanpentimento.com/crafts.htm
www.ewebtribe.com/NACulture/games.htm
fhss.byu.edu/anthro/mopc/pages/Education/EarthActivities/agames.htm
www.sierracanyon.pvt.k12.ca.us/school/chumash/games.html
www.nps.gov/bibe/teachers/lessonplans/cultural/amusements.htm
www.virtualmuseum.ca/Exhibitions/Traditions/index.html

Unit 4
Strategies

BEFORE READING

Preview the Selection

by looking at the photographs, illustrations, captions, and graphics to predict what the selection will be about.

DURING READING

Make Connections

by comparing my experiences with what I'm reading.

AFTER READING

Recall

by using the headings to question myself about what I read.

LEARN
the strategies
in the selection
The Great Salad Bowl
page 119

YOUR HERITAGE, OUR HERITAGE

PRACTICE
the **strategies**
in the selection
Many Lands, Many Breads
page 131

APPLY
the **strategies**
in the selection
Foods From the Americas:
A Shared Heritage
page 141

Think About
the
Strategies

BEFORE READING

Preview the Selection

by looking at the photographs, illustrations, captions, and graphics to predict what the selection will be about.

My Thinking

The strategy says to look at the photographs, illustrations, captions, and graphics to predict what the selection will be about. The illustrations show an adult and a child in the kitchen. The adult is cooking. I predict that this selection will be about cooking.

Also, the pictures show different foods, such as rice, spaghetti, and potatoes. There is also a list of ingredients for a recipe. This tells me that I will be reading about cooking some sort of meal.

I predict that this selection will be about food from other places. I'll read on to see if I'm right.

DURING READING

Make Connections

by comparing my experiences with what I'm reading.

My Thinking

The strategy says to compare my experiences with what I'm reading. I will stop and think about this strategy every time I come to a red button like this ⬤.

The Great Salad Bowl

"Grandma Rose, what smells so good?" Jonathan let the screen door slam shut behind him. Grandma Rose usually watched him after school. "What are you cooking?"

Grandma Rose scraped some small pieces of onion from her cutting board into a frying pan. They sizzled in hot peanut oil. "I'm making something special tonight, sweetie-pie! All the cousins are coming over. We're going to have all the foods my momma and daddy used to make back in **Jamaica**."

She sniffed and wiped her eyes on the corner of a dish towel—the onions had gotten to her. She pushed a strand of hair off her face with the back of her hand. "And you are coming, too!"

Vo·cab·u·lar·y

Jamaica (juh•**may**•kuh)— an island in the Caribbean

[119]

Jonathan looked at the foods Grandma Rose had put out to cook with. "Good!" he said. On the counter were a green bell pepper, a red bell pepper, a bottle of hot sauce, and, of course, the onion. These were foods Jonathan approved of. Jonathan's mouth began to water. But there were two bowls that contained things Jonathan hadn't seen before.

Learning About a New Food

"What's that lumpy yellow stuff?" Jonathan asked, wrinkling his nose. "And what's that white flaky stuff?"

"Well, Jonathan, those are the things this recipe is named for. It's called 'ackee and salt fish'." She picked up the bowl of yellow stuff. "This is the ackee. It's fruit from Africa that grows now in Jamaica. It's good." She paused to stir the onions. "This white stuff is codfish that's been salted and dried. I soaked it all night and all day to get the salt out."

Grandma Rose cut into the peppers and took out the seeds. Then she started dicing. "Once I get everything all cut up, I'll toss it all together in this frying pan until it's hot. It'll look like scrambled eggs—and taste like them, too!"

She wiped her hands and leaned against the counter-top. "When I was a little girl, we grew peppers and onions in our own yard. This was in **Kingston**. We could pick ackee from the trees out back of the house. You had to know just when the fruit was ripe or it would poison you! We liked knowing the ackee tree came from Africa just like we did."

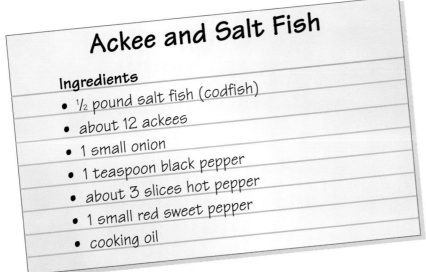

Ackee and Salt Fish

Ingredients

- ½ pound salt fish (codfish)
- about 12 ackees
- 1 small onion
- 1 teaspoon black pepper
- about 3 slices hot pepper
- 1 small red sweet pepper
- cooking oil

Can you buy all of these ingredients at your local store? Where else might you find them?

Strategy

Make Connections by comparing my experiences with what I'm reading.

My Thinking
This reminds me of being with my grandma. One time we found mushrooms on our walk. Grandma said that these mushrooms would be good for cooking. She showed me how to figure out if a mushroom is edible or poisonous. She warned me that most wild mushrooms are poisonous.

Learning About Yourself

The people living in the United States are like the parts of a great big tossed salad. A salad has many separate **ingredients**. Each one keeps its own flavor and color. But when put together, they make a whole new flavor that is very appealing. Every time new people arrive, they add new flavors and new ingredients.

Where did the first people living in the United States come from? People probably first came from Asia and spread throughout the Americas. This was thousands of years ago. Many of these people were probably the early ancestors of our present-day Native Americans. In the 1500s, European people started arriving. That started wave after wave of new arrivals. Today, many people are arriving from Mexico, Central America, and South America as well as from Asia and India.

Vo·cab·u·lar·y

Kingston (**king**•stuhn)— the capital of Jamaica

ingredients (in•**gree**•dee•uhnts)— the different foods and seasonings that make up a recipe

The United States is an exciting mix of people from all over the world. It is a salad bowl of people from many lands. Where did your family come from? What flavor does your family add to the salad bowl?

You can find out a lot about your roots by cooking and eating and talking about food. You can find out why your family eats certain foods. You can find out if the older people in your community grew up in the United States or if they came here from somewhere else. Ask them if they will share a meal or a recipe with you.

Finding out the favorite recipes of your family and your community is a good way to get to know your own history—the part you play in the salad bowl. Maybe you can fix a meal from an old recipe and invite some people from your community over to talk and eat with you. Or invite some of your friends over and share the foods of your culture with others.

Learning About Others

The next day, Jonathan was back. "Hi, Grandma Rose," he yelled. Again, he let the screen door slam shut behind him. Jonathan went right to the refrigerator. He opened the door and stuck his head inside.

"Let me guess," Grandma Rose said, coming into the room. "You're hungry!"

"I sure am," Jonathan said from inside the refrigerator. "And you must have some great leftovers from our **feast** last night!"

Vo·cab·u·lar·y

feast (feest)—a meal with lots of wonderful food

Make Connections
by comparing my experiences with what I'm reading.

My Thinking
One time I went to my friend's house, and we ate baklava for dessert. Her family came from Greece. They told me that this dessert is one of their Greek recipes.

They filled two bowls with the bright yellow salt fish and ackee and heated them in the microwave. "Grandma Rose?" Jonathan asked.

"Yes, Jonathan?" she replied.

"My friend Jake at school said that when his family gets together, they eat **shish kebabs** dipped in yogurt! His grandparents came from Turkey. And they eat other interesting stuff. He said I can come over and eat with them the next time they have a feast. Is that OK?"

"Of course it is, Jonathan," Grandma Rose said. "It's fun to learn about your own family's foods, but it's also fun to learn about other people's foods. Let's invite Jake over the next time the cousins get together." She took another bite of ackee. "OK?"

"OK!"

Vo·**cab**·u·lar·y

shish kebabs
(**shish** kuh•bobz)—a meat dish made by putting chunks of meat and vegetables on a long pointed stick and cooking them over a flame

Summary

The United States is made up of people from many parts of the world. How can cooking and eating together help you learn more about the history of your own family? Ask where the food came from originally. Find out from older family members and people in your community what they ate and how they cooked when they were younger. You may find that the things you eat every day go back to your family's roots around the world.

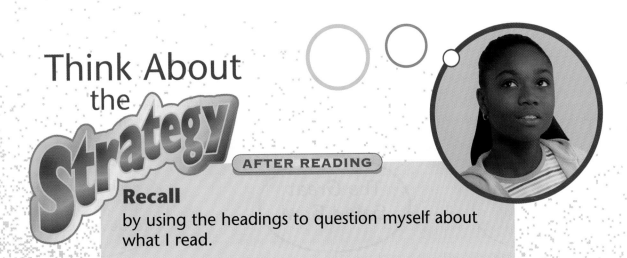

Think About the Strategy

AFTER READING

Recall

by using the headings to question myself about what I read.

My Thinking

The strategy says I should recall what I read by reading the headings. "Learning About a New Food" reminds me that the boy in the story learned about ackee and salt fish.

The next heading, "Learning About Yourself," reminds me that the United States is made up of many different people. I can learn about my family by observing the different things we eat and by cooking with my family.

Finally, "Learning About Others" reminds me that I can learn a lot from my friends, especially if their families came from different countries.

Graphic organizers help us organize information. I think this article can be organized by using a web. Here is how I organized the information. I put my central idea in the circle in the very middle. I used the subheadings in the three main circles attached to the middle circle. I put details about the subheadings in the circles attached to each of the main circles.

Web

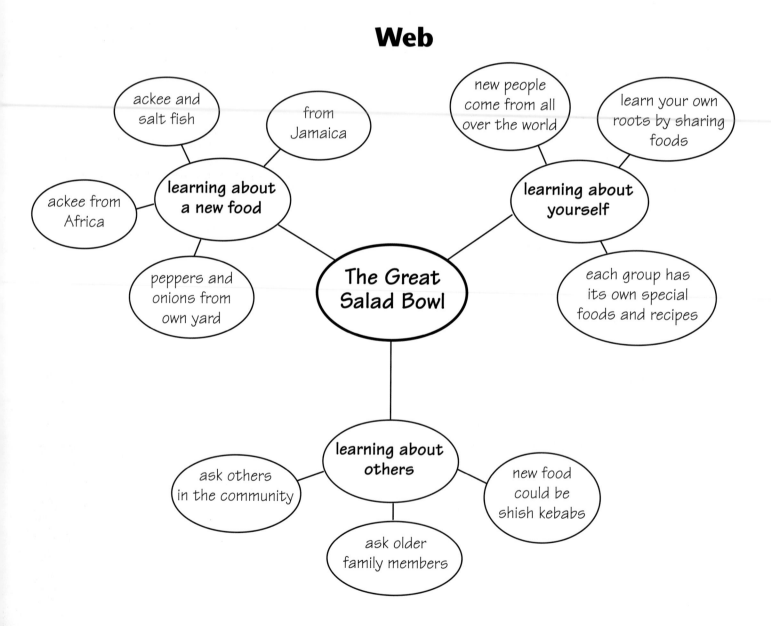

- ackee and salt fish
- from Jamaica
- ackee from Africa
- learning about a new food
- peppers and onions from own yard
- new people come from all over the world
- learn your own roots by sharing foods
- learning about yourself
- each group has its own special foods and recipes
- The Great Salad Bowl
- learning about others
- ask others in the community
- ask older family members
- new food could be shish kebabs

I used my graphic organizer to write a summary of the article. Can you find the information in my summary that came from my web?

A Summary of
The Great Salad Bowl

All the people in the United States can trace their families to other lands. Some people's ancestors lived in Asia thousands of years ago. Other people's families still live in other nations. When people move to the United States, they bring the food they like to eat. Food can help us learn about other people's families and our own families, as well. It's also fun to try new kinds of food.

What kinds of food does your family eat? Do you eat special dishes on certain holidays? Maybe your ancestors brought the recipes for these dishes with them when they came to the United States. Ask your family about each dish. You can learn about your own roots by learning more about the food you eat.

When you eat at a friend's house, is some of the food new to you? Your friend's ancestors might have brought the recipes from a land far away. If you ask about the food, you might learn interesting things about your friend's family.

Your own family can also try new foods from faraway places. Even if you never lived there, you can taste the food. You might try ackee and salt fish from Jamaica or shish kebabs from Turkey or the eastern Mediterranean area. You can take a vacation without leaving home!

Classmates and neighbors might name foods for you to try. You can learn about their families, too!

Introduction
Here is my introduction. It tells what I write about. The main idea is in the center of my web.

Body
I wrote one paragraph about each circle in my web.

Conclusion
I summarized my paper by recalling the main ideas.

Abbreviations

When following instructions like a recipe, a craft project, or a science lab, you need to pay attention to the measurements. Often the measurements are abbreviated, or shortened. Abbreviated words have some letters missing.

Here are common abbreviations for units of weight, volume, and length:

Measurement	Abbreviation	Measurement	Abbreviation
ounce	oz.	gallon	gal.
pound	lb.	milliliter	ml.
teaspoon	t. or tsp.	foot	ft.
tablespoon	T. or tbsp.	yard	yd.
fluid ounce	fl. oz.	meter	m.
quart	qt.	millimeter	mm.

The following sentences are instructions for different projects. On a separate sheet of paper, write the boldface abbreviation. Then write what the abbreviation stands for.

1. Mix 6 **fl. oz.** of corn syrup into the bowl of assorted-nuts.
2. Cut four 6-**ft.** pieces of wood for the shelves.
3. You will need a 1-**lb.** box of spiral pasta to make 2 wreaths.
4. The balsa wood used for the wings of the model plane should be 4 **mm.** thick.
5. To make the pattern, you will need 5 **yd.** of fabric.
6. For every 2 lemons, you should add 1 **qt.** of water and ½ **c.** of sugar.
7. Sprinkle 4 **tbsp.** of grated Parmesan cheese over the salad.
8. To paint the toy chest, you will need 1 **gal.** of purple paint.
9. Carefully measure 10 **ml.** of salt water, and pour it into the beaker.
10. Slowly add 6 **oz.** of melted chocolate into the bowl.

Readers' Theater

In the selection "The Great Salad Bowl," Jonathan told his Grandma Rose that he was invited to Jake's house for a feast. The script below tells what might have happened at that feast. Read the script aloud with a partner until you can read it with expression. When you are ready, perform it for the class.

TIP

Try to make this script sound like a conversation between Jonathan and Jake. What is Jonathan like? What is Jake like? Try to make their personalities come through in your reading.

Jonathan Eats at Jake's House

Jake: I'm so glad that you could come to our family feast!

Jonathan: Thanks for inviting me. I can't wait to try some of the foods you told me about.

Jake: Right! I'm hungry. Let's eat!

Jonathan: Great. What should I try first?

Jake: Try the shish kebabs. You're going to love them! My dad cooked these skewers of meat and vegetables outside on the grill. You can dip them in the yogurt sauce.

Jonathan: Mmmm, that is so good! What's this mushy stuff?

Jake: That is called babaganoush (bah•bah•guh•**noosh**). It's a spread made from roasted eggplant and garlic. You can spread it on the grilled pita (**pee**•tuh) bread.

Jonathan: What's pita bread?

Jake: Pita is thin, flat bread. We use it for spreads and sandwiches.

Jonathan: This food is so great. Thank you!

Jake: You're welcome. But don't fill up yet. Wait for dessert!

Jonathan: There's dessert, too!

Jake: Yup. My grandma makes great baklava (**bah**•kluh•vah). That's a pastry made with layers of phyllo (**fee**•loh) dough, honey, and crushed nuts. Phyllo is thin, buttery dough that gets crispy in the oven. Yum!

Jonathan: Yum is right! I wish my Grandma Rose could taste all of these fantastic foods. I know she'd love them.

Jake: Let's make you a plate of leftovers to take back to her. Then she can taste everything.

Jonathan: Great idea. Thanks!

Think About
the
Strategies

BEFORE READING

Preview the Selection
by looking at the photographs, illustrations, captions, and graphics to predict what the selection will be about.

 Write notes on your own paper to tell how you used this strategy.

DURING READING

Make Connections
by comparing my experiences with what I'm reading.

 When you come to a red button like this ⬤, write notes on your own paper to tell how you used this strategy.

[130]

Many Lands, Many Breads

Has anyone in your house ever made bread? Did the smell of the baking bread make your mouth water? Perhaps you make bread or **tortillas** at your house every day. Maybe there are breads that you eat only at special times of the year. For example, many Jewish people eat **matzo** crackers at Passover.

Bread has many names. It may be called **injera, lefse, pagach,** or pita. It depends on the culture that is doing the cooking.

There are hundreds of cultures in the world. There are similarities among them, and there are differences. For example, some groups respect Saturday as a day of rest and religious practice. Other people respect Friday, and still others honor Sunday. Some eat meat. Others are vegetarian. But almost every culture in the world eats some kind of bread.

Vo•cab•u•lar•y

tortillas (tor•**tee**•yuhz)—round, thin bread made in the Americas

matzo (**maht**•suh)—a bread eaten during the Jewish holiday of Passover; does not contain yeast

injera (in•**jair**•uh)—a round, flat bread eaten in Ethiopia

lefse (**lef**•suh)—a flat potato bread eaten in Norway

pagach (puh•**gahk**)—a Ukrainian filled bread

[131]

These grains can be ground into flour. They are often mixed with wheat flour and used to make a wide variety of breads.

Grains for Baking Breads

rye

wheat

crushed corn

millet

barley

rice

Different cultures make their bread with different grains. They cook their bread in different ways. They might make breads of different shapes. But they all make bread. Sometimes the bread is eaten alone. Often, it is used to hold other foods.

Have you ever eaten a peanut butter and jelly sandwich? If you have, then you're familiar with this use of bread. What other foods do you hold with bread?

The breads described here are just a few of the wonderful breads available in every community. See how many of them have you eaten. The next time you go grocery shopping, see how many different kinds of bread you can find.

Ethiopia: Injera

What country has bread that is similar to pancakes? The answer is Ethiopia [ee•thee•**oh**•pee•uh]. This is a country in the eastern part of Africa. In Ethiopia, the people make a type of bread called injera. Injera is made with a flour called teff. The word *teff* means "lost." It may be called this because the teff is so light that it is easily blown away. Teff is made from millet, a grain that has been grown in East Africa and the Middle East for thousands of years. To make injera, you combine teff with water and soda. This makes a thin batter.

Cooking injera is similar to cooking pancakes. First, a small amount of the batter is placed in a hot skillet. Then, the skillet is swirled around to spread the batter into a thin sheet. Soon the top of the batter starts to fill with bubbles. That's when the round bread is quickly removed from the skillet and set aside. The process is repeated until you have all the bread you need for a meal.

Injera is thin and **spongy**. When you eat Ethiopian food, you hold a piece of injera in your hand and pick up your other food with it.

Other foods from Ethiopia include spiced cheese, **lentils,** and doro wat [**dor**•oh waht] chicken, a dish made from chicken, onions, many different spices, and hard-boiled eggs. Tear off a piece of injera and dig right in!

Strategy

Make Connections by comparing my experiences with what I'm reading.

Write notes on your own paper to tell how you used this strategy.

Vo•cab•u•lar•y

spongy (**spun**•jee)—soft and full of holes, like a sponge

lentils (**len**•tulz)—flat beans common in the Middle East and Africa

[133]

Germany: Pumpernickel

Germany is a country in northern Europe. The German people make many kinds of bread, including pumpernickel. Pumpernickel is made with rye flour. Rye is a type of grain that is common in Europe. It has a much sharper flavor than wheat.

What other ingredients are in pumpernickel? A good recipe includes rye flour, whole-wheat flour, white flour, **yeast,** molasses, and cocoa powder. It seems funny to put cocoa powder in bread, but the cocoa helps give pumpernickel its rich taste as well as its color.

First, you mix the ingredients together in a big bowl. After the dough is mixed, you **knead** it. To knead the dough, you roll it and punch it with your hands, folding it over itself many times. Then you set the dough aside in a

Vo·cab·u·lar·y

yeast (yeest)—special fungus that produces gas bubbles that cause dough to enlarge, or rise

knead (need)—to mix, press, fold, and shape by hand

[134]

warm place for an hour. During the hour, the yeast causes the dough to expand, or rise. Then you knead the dough again and place it on a baking sheet that has been covered with cornmeal. The cornmeal keeps the bread from sticking to the pan.

After letting the dough rise again, you put the loaf into the oven. It smells great while it's baking. You end up with a dark, filling bread. It is wonderful to eat with soup or to hold a sandwich together. Warm pumpernickel with butter is delicious all by itself.

Strategy

Make Connections by comparing my experiences with what I'm reading.

Write notes on your own paper to tell how you used this strategy.

India: Chapati Bread

What kind of bread puffs up like a balloon? That's what happens to **chapati** from India. India is a large country in Asia. Many kinds of bread are made there. But chapati is one of the most interesting. The ingredients are simple. You need wholewheat flour, white flour, and warm water. The two flours and the water are blended together until a stiff dough is formed. Small pieces of the dough are pinched off. They are rolled into thin, round pieces about 8 inches across. These are placed on a hot **griddle** for only a few seconds.

Now comes the exciting part. After it leaves the griddle, the chapati is placed directly over an open gas flame. In just a few seconds, each piece of bread puffs up into a big ball! As it cools, it becomes flat again.

After cooking, the chapati is brushed with *ghee* [gee]. Ghee is a kind of butter used in many Indian dishes. This wonderful bread is used to pick up other foods in an Indian meal. Those foods might include **chutney** or

Vo•cab•u•lar•y

chapati (shuh•**paht**•ee)— a type of bread from India

griddle (**grid**•l)—a broad, flat cooking surface

chutney (**chut**•nee)—a thick sauce made from fruits and spices or vegetables and spices

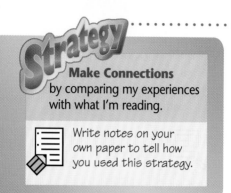

Strategy

Make Connections by comparing my experiences with what I'm reading.

Write notes on your own paper to tell how you used this strategy.

dal [dahl], a dish of peas or lentils cooked with spices. Or you might tear off a piece of chapati to scoop up some chicken *vindaloo* [**vin**•duh•loo]. This is a stew made with chicken, vegetables, and vindaloo, which is a mixture of 14 different spices. Enjoy!

United States: Cornbread

People from around the world have come to the United States. They bring their bread recipes with them. But were there any breads already in America?

One bread that comes from America is cornbread. Native Americans taught people from Europe how to grow and use corn. Fresh corn is cooked and eaten as a vegetable. Dried corn can be ground into a **coarse** flour called cornmeal. Cornbread is made from cornmeal.

You can make rough corn cakes with just cornmeal and water. Cornbread, however, is a little more complicated. A recipe for cornbread might include cornmeal, buttermilk, eggs, bacon fat, and small amounts of sugar, salt, and baking soda. These are mixed together to make a thick, gritty batter. The batter is poured into a hot greased skillet to cook on top of the stove. Or it may be baked in an oven. Wedges or squares of cornbread are often eaten with beans.

In the early days of our country, dry cornmeal and dried beans were very important. They were easy for travelers to carry, and they came to be eaten together. All people had to do was add water, and they had a satisfying meal.

Vo•cab•u•lar•y

coarse (kors)—rough in texture; gritty

Sometimes cornbread was crumbled right into the beans. Sometimes the beans were poured over pieces of the bread. Today, however, many people prefer cornbread by itself right out of the oven. They may have butter melting into it and maybe a dab of jelly on top.

People in every culture eat some form of bread. One culture may make a loaf that has to be sliced. Another may make flat round bread such as tortillas. Different grains are used to make different kinds of bread. In Ethiopia, teff is used in making injera. In Germany, rye flour is used to make pumpernickel. People in India use wheat and white flour to make chapati. And in the United States, cornmeal is used to make cornbread.

Strategy

Make Connections by comparing my experiences with what I'm reading.

Write notes on your own paper to tell how you used this strategy.

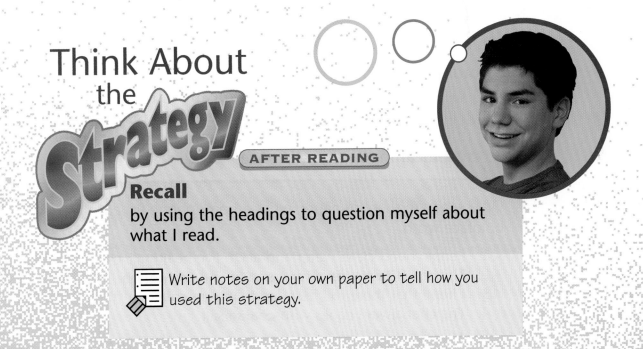

Think About the Strategy

AFTER READING

Recall by using the headings to question myself about what I read.

Write notes on your own paper to tell how you used this strategy.

Vocabulary

Homophones

Homophones are words that have the same pronunciation but different spellings and different meanings. For example, *two,* meaning "the number 2," and *too,* meaning "also," are homophones. Look at the spelling of a homophone and clues in the sentence to understand the word's meaning.

Read this passage from "Many Lands, Many Breads":

> *After the dough is mixed, you* **knead** *it. To* **knead** *the dough, you roll it and punch it with your hands, folding it over itself many times.*

What word sounds the same as *knead?* It's *need,* which means "something you must have." We can see from reading the sentences that the word *knead* has a different meaning, relating to how a person works with bread dough. *Knead* means "to mix, press, fold, and shape by hand."

Now look at another sentence from the selection:

> *Dried corn can be ground into a* **coarse** *flour called cornmeal.*

The words *coarse* and *course* are homophones. *Coarse* means "rough in texture; gritty." *Course* can mean "a part of a meal." The spelling, along with the context clues from the use of *corn* and *ground* in the sentence, suggest that "rough in texture; gritty" is the correct meaning in this sentence.

On a separate sheet of paper, write a homophone for each boldface word.

1. People **need** clean water and air to live healthy lives.
2. The baker always remembers to **knead** the dough.
3. I hope that there will be more than one **course** at this meal!
4. The chef always cooks with **coarse** salt.

On your sheet of paper, write a homophone for each word below. Then write the homophone's meaning. Use a dictionary if you need help.

5. beet	8. flour
6. eight	9. pear
7. bury	10. suite

Poetry

Practice reading this poem about bread several times until you can read it smoothly. Remember to pause at the commas. Then perform the poem with a partner.

Fluency **TIP**

> Reading with a partner can help develop your reading fluency. Read the poem several times with a partner (both of you reading the entire poem together at the same time). Try to adjust your voice to match your partner's while at the same time keeping the rhythm of the poem.

People Love Their Bread

Everywhere around the world
People love their bread.
They like it flat, they like it round,
With jam or plain instead.

Wheat and rye and plain old white
You'll find in many places.
Pita, matzah [**maht**•suh], and tortillas
Soon will join the races.

Corn, rice, oats, and spelt
Are very good bread flours.
Some breads are ready one, two, three
And some take many hours.

What's the favorite bread of all?
Ask anyone and see.
The bread that's best is always fresh,
Just made for you and me.

Think About the Strategies

Preview the Selection

by looking at the photographs, illustrations, captions, and graphics to predict what the selection will be about.

DURING READING

Make Connections

by comparing my experiences with what I'm reading.

AFTER READING

Recall

by using the headings to question myself about what I read.

 Use your own paper to jot notes to apply these Before, During, and After Reading Strategies. In this selection, you will choose when to stop, think, and respond.

Foods From the Americas:

A Shared Heritage

The **archaeologist** stepped back. She was digging in a certain place. She was using a paintbrush that was only an inch wide. She put it into a pocket on her tool belt. Then she pulled out a tiny artist's brush. Now was the time for careful work.

She knelt and skillfully brushed a tiny bit of soil at a time. She could see the **relic**. It was a small string bag. Her team had found several bags just like this one.

The archaeologist was working in Peru. It was a very old Inca burial place. The string bag was 1,000 years old. What was inside the burial bag?

Vo·**cab**·u·lar·y

archaeologist
(ahr·kee·**ol**·uh·jist)—
a scientist who studies the places where people lived long ago

relic (**rel**·ik)—a leftover from the distant past

She guessed that this small bag held what the others did. It would contain food. The Inca buried their dead with food to take into their next life.

Later that night, she was proved right. The bag held the foods that were most important to the Inca. It had peanuts, maize (corn), beans, and peppers.

You've no doubt eaten these foods. Native Americans developed these wonderful food crops. They were eating them long before Europeans came to the Americas.

The arrival of the Europeans brought changes. These foods began to travel. They were carried around the globe. Sailors from Spain, Portugal, England, and the Netherlands took part. They brought American foods to their homelands. They also took them to Africa, India, and Asia.

These foods made lasting changes. They changed how people of the world cooked and ate.

Where can the foods of the Americas be found today? They are part of almost every cooking tradition in the world. Check what you eat today! You may find that you're eating one of these foods.

The potato was developed as a food crop. This was high in the Andes mountains. It is cool and damp there. Potatoes were **domesticated** some 5,000 years ago.

A potato farmer inspects his crop.

The early **Peruvians** had potatoes of many sizes and colors. Their potatoes were white inside. But they had brown, purple, orange, or pink skins.

The Incas living in Peru depended on potatoes. Their word for potatoes was *papas* [**pah**•puhz]. They needed them to survive. Few other crops would grow on the steep mountains.

In the 1500s, Europeans came to know this as the potato. But they confused it with sweet potatoes. These were called *batatas* [buh•**tah**•tuhz]. They were eaten in the Caribbean.

The sweet potato caught on quickly in Europe. Why did the white potato take longer? Europeans thought it might cause disease. But by the 1800s, ideas changed.

Vo•cab•u•lar•y

domesticated
(duh•**mes**•ti•kayt•id)—made useful to humans

Peruvians
(puh•**roo**•vee•uhnz)—
the people who live in Peru

People around the world were eating potatoes.

How has the potato touched history? Potatoes grow well in the country of Ireland. People there came to depend on them. But in the middle 1800s, trouble began. Their crops began to die. The people had nothing to eat. Many of them died. Others left Ireland and came to the United States to live.

Many other people started moving to the United States, too. It was seen as a place of opportunity and freedom. The Irish were among the first groups to come in large numbers. And what did the Irish bring with them? They brought potato recipes, of course.

These are a few of the many kinds of potatoes you can buy.

Tomatoes

You are pouring ketchup on your burger. Are you thinking of ancient Mexico? That's where the tomato was developed. The tomato started thousands of years ago.

Spanish **invaders** moved into Mexico in 1519. They were the first people from outside the Americas to see the tomato. The **Aztec** people were eating several kinds of tomatoes.

Where does the word *tomato* come from? It comes from the Aztec word *tomatl* [toh•**mah**•tl]. These early tomatoes were different. They were not like the big, shiny, red tomatoes we eat today. They were smaller and not as round.

The Spanish took tomato plants back to Europe. They were grown as **decorative** plants! The Europeans had never seen anything like them. No one knew how to cook them. Europeans were also afraid that tomatoes might be poisonous.

Vo•cab•u•lar•y

invaders (in•**vayd**•uhrz)—people who move into a country with the purpose of controlling it or taking its goods

Aztec (**az**•tek)—people living in Mexico 500 years ago

decorative (**dek**•uhr•uh•tiv)—grown or owned only for beauty, not for food

[**143**]

There are many different kinds of tomatoes.

Spain and Italy accepted the tomato more quickly than other European countries did. Today, much of southern Italian cooking depends on the tomato.

India and countries in Africa also adopted the tomato. It is the most common fruit grown in China.

And, of course, the love of tomatoes and foods made with tomatoes continues to grow in the United States. What else do you eat that contains tomatoes or tomato sauce?

Peppers

Peppers—sweet, hot, green, chili, and **cayenne**—were grown throughout the Americas. This was well before the Europeans came in the 1500s. These foods were spicy. The Europeans called them "peppers." Black pepper was one of the main spices used in Europe at that time.

Caribbean people called the fruits of these plants *aji* [ah•hee]. The Aztecs in Mexico called them *chilis* [**chee**•leez]. This word is still associated with chili peppers.

Where did hot peppers first become popular? Europeans found American peppers to be too hot. But people in Asia and Africa loved them. American peppers are an important part of many cooking traditions. Indian, Chinese, Thai, and many African cooks use peppers.

In those countries, many people love peppers. They believe that peppers have always grown there. They are not aware that the foods came from the Americas.

American peppers began to arrive in Europe from Africa and Asia. Then they began to be accepted. That added to the confusion. People were not sure where these vegetables really came from.

In the late 1900s, immigrants to the United States brought America's peppers back home. They came from places such as Mexico, Thailand, India, and Vietnam. They are very popular today. And some people think "the hotter, the better."

Spicy salsa is made with peppers. It is the most popular sauce in the United States. It has even replaced ketchup!

Maize (Corn)

What was the most important food taken from the Americas? It is maize. Maize comes from the **Arawak**

Vo•cab•u•lar•y

cayenne (ky•**en**)—a type of hot pepper

Arawak (**air**•uh•wahk)—people living in the Caribbean in the 1500s

[144]

word *mahiz* [**mah**•heez]. It is commonly called corn. Maize spread around the world.

American peoples grew different types of corn. They used it in many ways. They boiled it and roasted it. They made tortillas from it. They even had a kind of beer made from it.

Corn started as a wild grass in Mexico. That was at least 8,000 years ago. By 1,000 years ago, it was a food. It was being grown throughout North, South, and Central America. In 1621, the **Wampanoag** Indians helped the English **Pilgrims**. They taught them how to grow and cook corn. Corn kept the Pilgrims from starving to death.

Maize grows more quickly than wheat. It also has more **nutrients** in it than wheat. In southern Europe, many people owned tiny plots of land. Corn became popular there. In countries of Africa, corn was adopted quickly. People in **Ghana** and **Congo** eat corn mush.

Many people enjoy eating different kinds of sweet corn.

Recipes for corn returned to the Americas. Enslaved Africans brought them to the American South.

People in African countries and in India and China think peppers are a native food. They also think of maize as their own. They think so because they have eaten it since early times.

Have you had any foods made with maize today? Check the labels before you answer. Corn syrup is used in many foods that don't seem to contain corn.

Foods from the Americas have spread around the world. When Europeans first arrived in the Americas, the people living here were eating strange new foods. They were potatoes, tomatoes, peppers, and corn. People ate beans, peanuts, and chocolate, as well.

These were foods the Europeans had never seen before. The Europeans took the foods back to Europe. They also carried these foods around the world. They became part of the diet of many different countries and cultures.

Many of these foods returned to the Americas in new recipes. People from other countries moved to the United States. They brought the foods with them.

Spaghetti? Curry? Putu? The ancient Americans didn't eat these dishes. But they knew many of the ingredients. They are part of a food heritage shared by the world.

Vo•cab•u•lar•y

Wampanoag (wam•puh•**noh**•ahg)—people living in part of New England in the 1600s

Pilgrims (**pil**•gruhmz)— a group of people from England who settled in Massachusetts in the 1620s

nutrients (**noo**•tree•uhnts)— the parts of food that are good for us

Ghana (**gah**•nuh)—a country in West Africa

Congo (**kong**•goh)— a country in Central Africa

Vocabulary

Idioms

An **idiom** is "a commonly used expression or phrase that means something different from what it appears to mean." Many idioms relate to food. For example, if something is "a piece of cake," it is easy.

Here is another example.

> *Sara is a caring, thoughtful, and responsible person. Her teacher says that she is a* **good egg***.*

The expression "good egg" is an idiom because it would not make sense for Sarah's teacher to call her an egg. The context clues, *thoughtful* and *responsible,* in the first sentence suggest that *good egg* means "a good person."

Let's look at one more example:

> *We can't finish the project without complete ideas. Those ideas are* **half-baked***.*

You can tell that *half-baked* is an idiom because ideas are not *baked.* You can find the meaning of this idiom by looking at the surrounding words first. The writer is comparing *half-baked* foods (foods that are not fully cooked) to *half-baked* ideas. The writer says they need "complete ideas." The idiom *half-baked* means "not thought out or studied carefully."

Read the sentences below. Use context clues to find the meaning of each idiom in boldface. Write each idiom and its meaning on a separate sheet of paper. Discuss your answers with a partner.

1. We talked for a long time, but we really didn't say much. **In a nutshell**, she told me that she's moving.
2. Stay quiet! Don't **spill the beans** about Mom's surprise party!
3. I hate walking in the rain. It is not my **cup of tea**.
4. When you take a test, don't get upset. Try to stay **as cool as a cucumber**.
5. Dad works hard to make money. He really **brings home the bacon**.

Silly Story

Read the silly story several times. Look for the idioms, and think about what they mean. Remember to read sentences punctuated with exclamation points with excitement. When you feel ready, perform the story for a partner.

Fluency TIP

As you practice reading this story, try to emphasize the food idioms in order to highlight them for the listening audience.

A Corny Story

When I came home from school the other day, I was so hungry I could have eaten a horse!

"What's for dinner?" I asked my brother Miguel.

"Who knows?" he said. "Mom's still at work. Someone has to bring home the bacon."

"Let's make dinner," I said. "It'll be as easy as pie!"

"No way! Cooking is not my cup of tea," said Miguel.

I really needed Miguel's help. So I tried to butter him up.

"Miguel, you are the apple of my eye," I said.

"OK, Shelly, I'll help you with dinner," Miguel replied. It worked! "But the cooking better be a piece of cake!" he added.

"Cooking isn't hard!" I told him. "All you have to do is use your noodle and stay cool as a cucumber."

In a nutshell, Miguel and I made a delicious meal.

"Mmmm," said Miguel. "This food is the cream of the crop!"

Mom was pleased, too. "You kids take the cake!" she declared.

Map

How Many People Come From Other Nations?

Many people were born in other nations and moved to the United States. You can see where they live now on this map. Some states have many people from other nations. Some states have only a few. The colors show how many people out of every 100 were born in another nation. The legend explains what each color means.

about 1 to 3 people out of every 100 were born in another nation

about 4 to 6 people out of every 100

about 7 to 10 people out of every 100

about 11 to 16 people out of every 100

about 17 to 26 people out of every 100

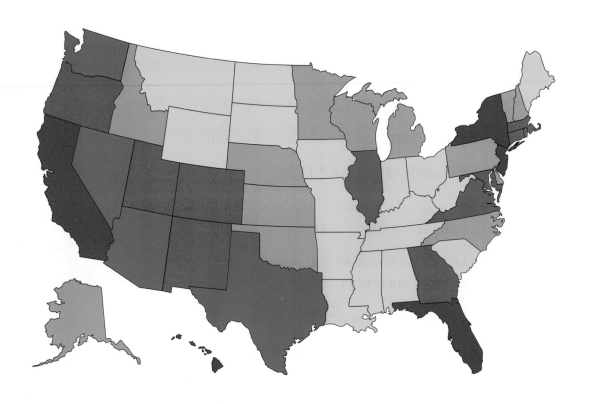

Discussion Questions

Answer these questions with a partner or on a separate sheet of paper.

1. Which state below has the fewest people who were born in another nation?
   a. Maine
   b. Illinois
   c. Texas
   d. Oregon

2. Name three states in which at least 17 of every 100 people were born in another nation.

3. Look at the map. Which sentence best describes the Southwest?
   a. Very few people in the Southwest were born in other nations.
   b. Most people in the Southwest were born in other nations.
   c. The Southwest has more people from other nations than any other region of the United States.
   d. The Southwest has fewer people from other nations than any other region of the United States.

4. This map was made in 2000. Back then, how many people in your state were born in another nation?

5. Do you think the number of people in your state from other nations has increased or decreased since 2000? Explain your answer.

6. What would this map be like 200 years ago, when the United States was still being settled?
   a. Most states would have few people born in other nations.
   b. Most states would have many people born in other nations.
   c. The states on the East Coast would have few people born in other nations.
   d. The map would look much like it does today.

7. Why do you think people from other nations want to move to the United States?
   a. They want more freedom than they have in their own nation.
   b. They want better jobs and better lives for their families.
   c. They want to go to college here and then return to their own nations.
   d. All of these reasons

8. What are two problems that people often face when they move here from other nations?

Family Foods

Choose a food that is part of your family's tradition. Gather information about it, such as where it started; how or where it is available; and how it looks, smells, and tastes. Prepare a written, oral, or visual presentation about that food to share with the class.

We Eat Bread

Poll your classmates to learn the kinds of bread they have eaten. Summarize your findings, indicating how many students named each kind of bread. Present the information as a visual display.

Write a Letter

Imagine you are with one of the early explorers to the Americas. You observe people eating a food you have never seen or heard of before. You decide to try some of this food. Write a letter to someone back home in Europe. Name the food, and describe what it looks, feels, smells, and tastes like. Include your opinion about how this food might be accepted back in your hometown.

Class Recipes

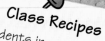

Invite other students in your class to help you develop a class collection of recipes for foods from different cultures and ethnicities. Have students check with family members to find one or more recipes. Use standard recipe cards, and have students write or type the recipes for a class collection. Remind them to include all the needed ingredients and the directions for making the food. Display the cards on a bulletin board where other students can find and copy a card for a food they would like to try.

Foods From Other Places

On a large map of the world, prepare a presentation of the foods covered in this unit. Using photographs or handmade pictures of each food, attach the images to the map. Use string or yarn to stretch between the food and the country of its origin. Be sure to label each food item.

A Different Kind of Store

Make arrangements to visit a bakery or store in your area that makes or sells products of certain ethnicities. Report back to the class about what you learned. Your report could be oral or written.

Related Books

Dupaigne, Bernard. *The History of Bread.* Harry N. Abrams, Inc., 1999.

Fabricant, Florence. *The Great Potato Book.* Ten Speed Press, 2001.

Harbison, Elizabeth M. *Loaves of Fun: A History of Bread With Activities and Recipes From Around the World.* Chicago Review Press, 1997.

Hill, Mary. *Let's Make Bread.* Children's Press, 2002.

Johnson, Sylvia A. *Tomatoes, Potatoes, Corn, and Beans: How the Foods of the Americas Changed Eating Around the World.* Atheneum Books for Young Readers, 1997.

Jones, Carol. *Bread.* Chelsea House Publishers, 2002.

Klingel, Cynthia, and Robert B. Noyed. *Bread and Cereal.* Weekly Reader Early Learning Library, 2002.

Llewellyn, Claire. *Bread.* Children's Press, 1999.

Meltzer, Milton. *The Amazing Potato: A Story in Which the Incas, Conquistadors, Marie Antoinette, Thomas Jefferson, Wars, Famines, Immigrants, and French Fries All Play a Part.* HarperCollins Publishers, 1992.

Mitchell, Melanie. *Life Cycles: Potatoes.* Lerner Publications Company, 2003.

Spilsbury, Louise. *Potatoes.* Heinemann Library, 2001.

Interesting Web Sites

To find out more about the foods in this unit, visit these sites.

http://www.agric.gov.ab.ca/agdex/potato/growing1.html

http://www.pastrywiz.com/letseat/

http://www.smm.org/sln/tf/b/bread/bread.html

http://www.foodland.gov.on.ca/facts/potato_2002.htm

http://collections.ic.gc.ca/potato/index.asp

http://www.potatohelp.com/

http://www.botham.co.uk/seed/first.htm

http://www.botham.co.uk/bread/history1.htm

http://www.canadianpoppingcorn.com/cornhistory.html

http://www.nativetech.org/cornhusk/cornhusk.html

http://www.breadwithoutborders.com/site/526210/page/135134

http://waltonfeed.net/self/grains.html

Unit 5

Strategies

BEFORE READING

Activate Prior Knowledge

by reading the introduction and/or summary to decide what I know about this topic.

DURING READING

Interact With Text

by identifying how the text is organized.

AFTER READING

Evaluate

by forming a judgment about whether the selection was objective or biased.

LEARN
the *strategies*
in the selection
Reaching the Peak
page 155

PRACTICE
the *strategies*
in the selection
Earhart's Adventures
page 167

APPLY
the *strategies*
in the selection
Pole Position
page 177

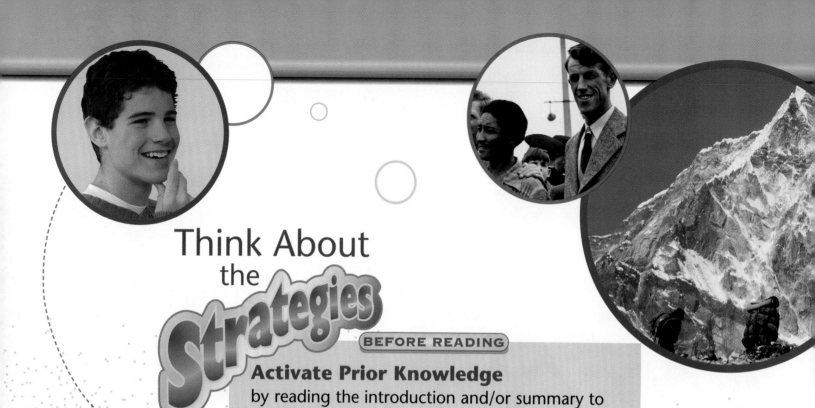

Think About
the
Strategies

Activate Prior Knowledge

by reading the introduction and/or summary to decide what I know about this topic.

My Thinking

The strategy says to activate prior knowledge by reading the introduction and/or summary to decide what I know about this topic. Well, the introduction talks about Mount Everest. It tells about how high the mountain is compared with the Sears Tower. And it tells who the first people were to climb to the peak.

I already know that Mount Everest is the highest mountain on earth. And I know people have been to the top and lived to tell about it. But I wasn't sure who the first ones were, and I don't really know much about their trip. Now I can read on to find out.

DURING READING

Interact With Text

by identifying how the text is organized.

My Thinking

The strategy says to interact with text by identifying how the text is organized. I will stop and think about this strategy every time I come to a red button like this ⦿.

Reaching the Peak

The peak of Mount Everest reaches higher than any other place on earth.

Introduction

What is the highest place you've ever been? Maybe you've been high in the Rocky Mountains. Or you went to the **observation deck** of the Sears Tower in Chicago. Those are pretty high places. But compared with the highest point on earth they seem very small. The highest point on earth is the top of Mount Everest. It is on the border of Tibet [tuh•**bet**] and Nepal [nuh•**pawl**] in Asia. It is 29,035 feet tall. It reaches nearly five and one-half miles into the sky.

You can get to the top of the Sears Tower (1,800 feet high) by walking into an elevator. You just push the "up" button. Getting to the top of Mount Everest is a lot harder. That's what Sir Edmund Hillary and Tenzing Norgay found out. They were the first people to reach the peak and return to tell about their adventure.

Vo•**cab**•u•lar•y

observation deck
(ob•zuhr•**vay**•shuhn dek)—
an area near the top of a tall building for looking out

[155]

Vo•**cab**•u•lar•y

Ruapehu
(roo•uh•**pay**•hoo)—the highest mountain in New Zealand

expedition
(ek•spi•**dish**•uhn)—a journey undertaken for a specific purpose, often an adventure or scientific mission

Who Were Hillary and Norgay?

Sir Edmund Hillary was born in New Zealand in 1919. His family raised bees and farmed. New Zealand has many mountains. But Hillary's family was busy making a living. It wasn't until he was 16 years old that Hillary first saw a mountain, Mount **Ruapehu**. It is north of Wellington [**wel**•ing•tuhn], the capital of New Zealand.

It was love at first sight. He loved the snow. He loved the challenge of the climb. He loved the feeling of freedom he got standing at the top of a mountain peak. From then on, Hillary climbed whenever he could. Right after World War II, he and Harry Ayres climbed Mount Cook in New Zealand. They were the first to climb that peak's southern ridge.

Less is known about Tenzing Norgay. Norgay supervised the **expedition** to climb Mount Everest. He and Hillary became good friends.

The Sherpas

Norgay was a Sherpa. Sherpas are a group of people who have always lived in the Himalayas. This is the mountain chain where Mount Everest is located. Without the knowledge and strength of Sherpa guides and assistants, climbing Mount Everest would no doubt be impossible.

These climbers are working their way up Mount Everest.

Have you ever tried to carry a heavy box up a hill or up a flight of stairs? If so, then you know how strong the Sherpas must be. They carry supplies up the world's highest mountain. Sherpas lay the trail and carry supplies. The area is so high that no motor-powered vehicles, such as trucks, can function.

A motor needs **oxygen**. This gas mixes with fuel. It causes combustion to get the motor started and to keep it running. There's not enough oxygen at the top of Mount Everest to do this. Even helicopters are unable to fly there. The air is so thin that the blades have nothing to push against to keep the helicopter in the sky. The power behind an **ascent** of Everest is muscle power.

Plant Life on Mount Everest

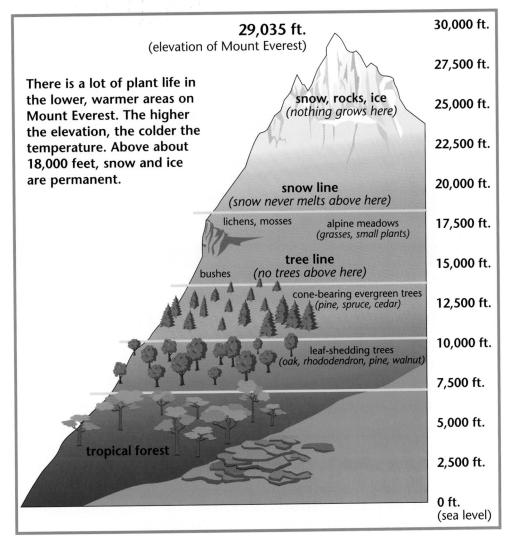

29,035 ft.
(elevation of Mount Everest)

There is a lot of plant life in the lower, warmer areas on Mount Everest. The higher the elevation, the colder the temperature. Above about 18,000 feet, snow and ice are permanent.

30,000 ft.

27,500 ft.

snow, rocks, ice
(nothing grows here)

25,000 ft.

22,500 ft.

snow line
(snow never melts above here)

20,000 ft.

lichens, mosses   alpine meadows
(grasses, small plants)

17,500 ft.

tree line
(no trees above here)

15,000 ft.

bushes

cone-bearing evergreen trees
(pine, spruce, cedar)

12,500 ft.

leaf-shedding trees
(oak, rhododendron, pine, walnut)

10,000 ft.

7,500 ft.

5,000 ft.

tropical forest

2,500 ft.

0 ft.
(sea level)

Vo·**cab**·u·lar·y

oxygen (ok•si•juhn)— the part of the air that your body uses to stay alive

ascent (uh•**sent**)—an upward movement or climb

Climbing Everest

Hillary was in his early thirties. He took part in many climbing trips in the Himalayas. All were in preparation to climb Mount Everest. In 1953, he made the attempt. A British expedition was going to make the climb.

It took weeks of hiking just to get to Everest. Several hundred **porters** carried gear. At about 13,000 feet, they crossed the tree line. That's the point so high that trees can no longer grow. There is nothing to provide shelter from the wind and cold.

The team rests on the long trek up Mount Everest.

The Nuts and Bolts—Or Ropes and Crampons

How does climbing a tall mountain affect your body? At a high **altitude,** the oxygen in the air thins out. This makes it difficult to breathe. Snowy slopes and icy cliffs rise up in front of you. They make it difficult to find and keep a foothold.

The temperature drops quickly to many degrees below zero. Fierce winds whip around you. These were the challenges Hillary and his group faced. They could fall, freeze to death, or die of **altitude sickness**. Or they could simply wander off the trail, never to be seen again.

Vo·cab·u·lar·y

porters (**por**•tuhrz)—persons hired to carry equipment and supplies

altitude (**al**•ti•tood)—how high above sea level a location is

altitude sickness—an illness that occurs at high altitudes when the body does not get enough oxygen

That's what happened to climbers George Mallory and Andrew Irvine. They were on an expedition in 1924. No one knows whether they reached the top. They simply disappeared. Seventy-five years later, in 1999, Mallory's frozen body was found. From the place where he died, many climbers think that he did not reach the top. But a clear answer has not yet been found. ●················

Mallory and Irvine may have reached the peak. That would mean that Hillary and Norgay were not the first people to stand on the top of Everest. The history books—and this article—would have to be rewritten.

Everything about the expedition had to be planned with great care. Which route would they take up the mountain? How many oxygen tanks would they need to carry?

Special gear, such as crampons and ice axes, was needed. Crampons are sharp spikes that attach to climbing boots. They give climbers a better grip on ice and snow. Ropes are tied carefully between climbers. The ropes are anchored to handholds and rocks to keep climbers from falling.

Ice axes are used to chip handholds in the ice. Climbers also use ice axes to stop themselves if they start sliding down a field of snow. Digging in with the point of the ax slows climbers down enough to get back on their feet.

A climber uses crampons and ice axes to climb these snow-covered peaks.

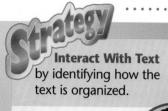

Strategy

Interact With Text
by identifying how the
text is organized.

My Thinking
I was right. The
selection is telling
the order of
events in Hillary's
climb. I think this is called
"sequence of events."

Vo·cab·u·lar·y

phase (fayz)—a stage or step

oxygen masks—masks that
are connected to a tank of
oxygen; used to assist in
breathing in places where
there is not enough oxygen

summit (sum•it)—the top
of a mountain

Making the Ascent

Slowly, the climbers worked their way across the icefall.
This is a dangerous glacier. They set up eight camps above
the icefall. Each was at a higher altitude. They would
climb from one camp to the next. Climbers would rest at
each one for several weeks. This would allow their bodies
to get used to the new, higher altitude. This **phase** of the
climb took months.

From Camp 8, two-person teams would try to reach the
top of the mountain. Hillary and Norgay were to be the
second team to make the attempt. How did they get to be
the first to try for the top? It happened when the first
team's oxygen tanks failed to operate.

Suddenly, Hillary and Norgay had their chance. They
would be the very first to see the world from its highest
point. They would be on the top of Mount Everest. On
May 29, 1953, from a camp even higher than Camp 8, they
started out.

The climbers wore **oxygen masks** and crampons. They
climbed over snow and ice. They came to a 40-foot cliff.
Hillary almost turned back. They had to get to the **summit**
and back as quickly as possible. His legs felt as heavy as
iron. But his dream of reaching the peak spurred him on.

He wedged
himself between
the ice and the
cliff. Slowly he
crept up the
crack an inch at
a time. Finally,
he was out of the
crack! But ahead
of him was more
ice! Would they
ever reach the
topmost point?
Hillary was
trudging across
the ice. Then he
became aware
of something.

People cheer for Hillary and Norgay after the
climb. Norgay is holding the flag, and Hillary is
on the right.

The ice was starting to slant down instead of up. They had made it to the peak!

Hillary and Norgay shook hands. They planted a flag and took some pictures. Then they got down from there as quickly as they could!

A Dream Fulfilled

What did Edmund Hillary do after he made his dream come true? He dreamed more dreams. He worked to make them come true. He continued climbing for many years. He made a trip across Antarctica to the South Pole. He toured the world, telling people about his adventures.

Hillary also worked hard and raised a lot of money. His plan was to help the people of Nepal and Tibet. He helped them build schools, hospitals, roads, and airstrips. There are many controversies today about climbing Mount Everest. But no one questions Hillary and Norgay's **momentous** achievement.

Vo·cab·u·lar·y

momentous
(moh•**men**•tuhs)—important

Think About the Strategy

AFTER READING

Evaluate
by forming a judgment about whether the selection was objective or biased.

My Thinking

The strategy says that I should evaluate by forming a judgment about whether the selection was objective or biased. That means I need to decide. I think it was objective because it told the story in the right order of how it happened. It told about the dangers and the need for careful preparations. It even told about another team that died trying to climb the same mountain. It was interesting when the writer said that if the other team did reach the top, history books would have to be rewritten. But since nobody knows for sure, then Hillary's team was the first.

Graphic organizers help us organize information. A time line is a graph that shows events happening in order of time. Time lines show which event happened first, which came—in order—next, and which happened last. Notice how the time line helped me when I wrote my summary, on the next page.

Time Line
Reaching the Peak

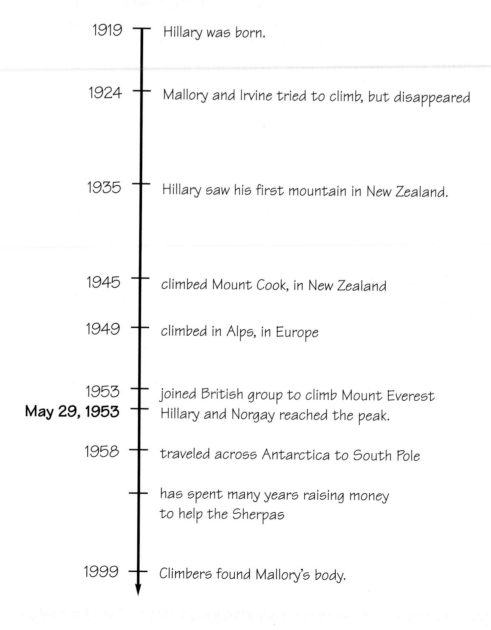

1919	Hillary was born.
1924	Mallory and Irvine tried to climb, but disappeared
1935	Hillary saw his first mountain in New Zealand.
1945	climbed Mount Cook, in New Zealand
1949	climbed in Alps, in Europe
1953	joined British group to climb Mount Everest
May 29, 1953	Hillary and Norgay reached the peak.
1958	traveled across Antarctica to South Pole
	has spent many years raising money to help the Sherpas
1999	Climbers found Mallory's body.

I used my graphic organizer to write a summary of the article. Can you find the information in my summary that came from my time line?

A Summary of
Reaching the Peak

Sir Edmund Hillary loved mountains most of his life. He was born in New Zealand in 1919. In 1924, Hillary was five years old. He had not yet seen a mountain. Still, something happened that would affect his life. Two climbers named George Mallory and Andrew Irvine disappeared. They had been trying to climb Mount Everest. It is the highest point on earth.

In 1935, when Hillary was 16, he saw his first mountain. He fell in love with climbing. From then on, Hillary climbed whenever he could. Soon after World War II, he and a friend were the first to climb Mount Cook. It is in New Zealand.

In 1953, Hillary joined a group of British climbers. They were trying to climb Mount Everest. After months of climbing, Hillary and Tenzing Norgay were the first to reach the peak. The date was May 29, 1953. Norgay was a Sherpa. The Sherpas live in the mountains and guide climbers.

In 1999, other climbers found Mallory's body. He was on Everest. Still, Mallory and Irvine probably did not reach the peak. That means Hillary and Norgay were the first to get there.

Hillary climbed mountains for many more years. He told people about his adventures. He also raised money to help others, especially the people in Nepal and Tibet. Hillary never lost his love for climbing.

Introduction
Here is my introduction. It tells what I will write about. The main idea is the title of my time line.

Body
I used information from the dates in my time line for the paragraphs in my body copy. The time line helped me write about Hillary in time order.

Conclusion
I summarized my paper by recalling the last part of my time line.

Vocabulary

Antonyms

Antonyms are words that have opposite meanings. Antonyms are also the same part of speech. For example, *hot* and *cold* are antonyms. They have opposite meanings, and they are both adjectives.

Read this sentence from the selection "Reaching the Peak":

> *The power behind an **ascent** of Everest is muscle power.*

The word **ascent** is a noun that means "an upward movement." The word **descent** is an antonym of *ascent*. **Descent** is also a noun. It means "a downward movement." Read a sentence with both *ascent* and *descent*:

> *The climbers found the **descent** to be easier than the **ascent**.*

Ascend is a verb that comes from the same root as *ascent*. It means "to move or go up." Can you think of an antonym of *ascend*? If you said *descend*, you're right! *Descend* is also a verb. It means "to move or go down."

You can find antonyms in a thesaurus. A thesaurus is like a dictionary, but instead of definitions, it lists synonyms and antonyms of words. (Remember, synonyms are words with the same or similar meanings.)

> Think of an antonym for each boldface word below. On a separate sheet of paper, write the antonym. Then write a sentence that includes that antonym. Remember to make sure that the words are the same part of speech. Use a dictionary or a thesaurus if you need help.
>
> 1. The elephant is the **strongest** animal in the circus.
>
> 2. The room was **quieter** after we turned off the television.
>
> 3. Setting up the tent was **easy** after we read the directions.
>
> 4. She wasn't very hungry, so she ate a **light** lunch.
>
> 5. If we all agree to the plans, we can **begin** getting ready for the party.

Readers' Theater

The following script is a fictional conversation between Tenzing Norgay and Sir Edmund Hillary as they leave Camp 8 to climb to the summit of Mount Everest. Practice reading this script aloud with a partner. When you are ready, perform it for an audience.

Fluency TIP

Hillary was the leader of the expedition, and Norgay was a guide. Try to make your reading reflect the characters' personalities and positions as you read each part.

Hillary and Norgay on Top of the Earth

Norgay: It's been a lot of hard work and long planning, but we're almost there. Are you ready to set out?

Hillary: As ready as I'll ever be! Today we'll reach the very top, and we will make history!

Norgay: Yes, but we will need to keep a sure and steady pace up to the summit. We have made it this far with good planning and determination. We will not give up now.

Hillary: Just imagine! You and I will be standing at the highest place on earth!

Norgay: It will be an extraordinary accomplishment.

Hillary: It will be the fulfillment of our dreams.

Norgay: Let's review the plan. We must not stay long at the summit. There is always the danger that our oxygen tanks could fail.

Hillary: Yes, we'll be careful and safe. Not only do we have to make it to the summit safely, but we also have to make it back to base camp. We have to make it back because we'll have so many stories to tell!

Think About
the
Strategies

BEFORE READING

Activate Prior Knowledge
by reading the introduction and/or summary to decide what I know about this topic.

 Write notes on your own paper to tell how you used this strategy.

DURING READING

Interact With Text
by identifying how the text is organized.

 When you come to a red button like this ⊙, write notes on your own paper to tell how you used this strategy.

Earhart's Adventures

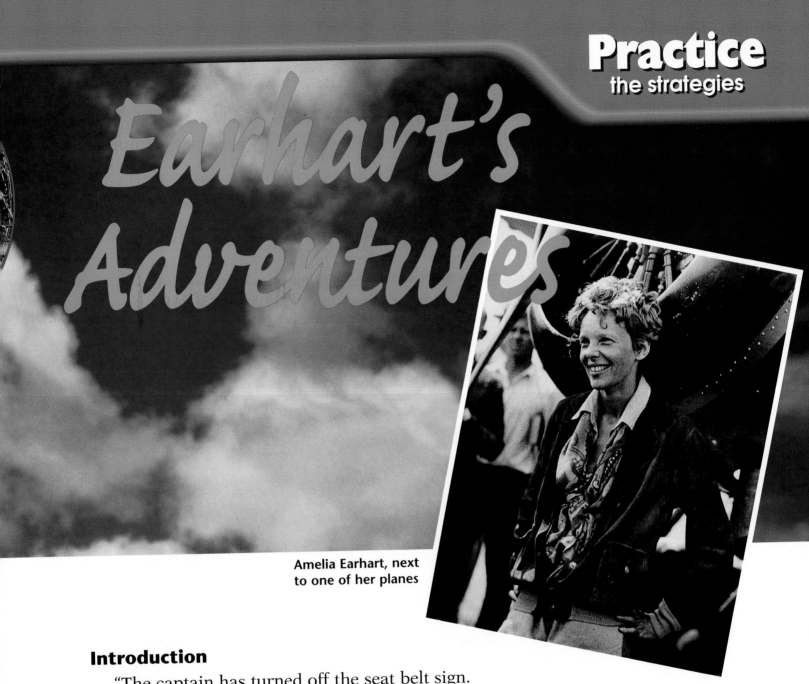

Amelia Earhart, next to one of her planes

Introduction

"The captain has turned off the seat belt sign. Feel free to move around the cabin."

This is about as exciting as air travel gets for most people. They strap into seats and arrive where they're going. It's all so smooth that it doesn't feel much like flying. Things were different for Amelia Earhart.

Earhart was a pilot in the early days of **aviation**. She flew in open planes. She could feel the wind stream past her face. She could see the earth rush up to meet her when she landed. She spent half of her life following her dreams of flying. And she disappeared mysteriously in 1937.

Vo•cab•u•lar•y

aviation (ay•vee•**ay**•shuhn)—the operation of heavier-than-air aircraft

The Dream Is Born

Earhart was a pioneer of aviation. She was born in Atchison, Kansas, on July 24, 1897. She loved adventure and travel. This was true even when she was a young girl.

One story tells of how Earhart and her sister built a roller coaster. It was on the roof of a shed. The crash landing didn't bother her a bit! Have you ever tried anything so daring?

Earhart graduated from high school in Chicago in 1915. Soon after that, she traveled to Toronto, Ontario. She worked as a nurse's aide during World War I (1914–1918). That's where her dream of being a pilot was born.

Amelia Earhart in Honolulu, Hawaii, working on her plane

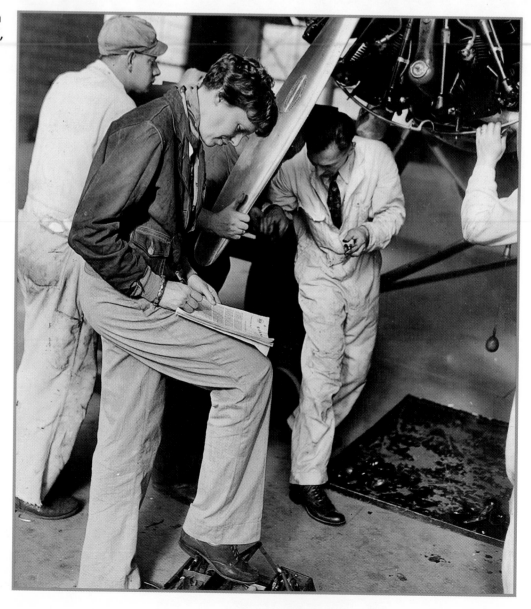

She went to college for a little while. But the dream of flying was stronger than her dream of becoming a doctor. She left college and moved to California. In California, she worked at a telephone company. She paid for flying lessons. And she saved enough money to buy her own airplane!

Strategy

Interact With Text by identifying how the text is organized.

Write notes on your own paper to tell how you used this strategy.

Earhart's Plane

Have you ever flown in an airplane? You may have flown in a large jet. It may have seated hundreds of people. But the single-engine planes in which Earhart learned her piloting skills were different. They were small, **fragile** machines. They were built of metal or wood frames. These were covered with canvas or sheet metal.

The cockpit, the part of the plane holding the pilot, was open to the sky. Pilots wore heavy jackets, goggles, and scarves. They had to protect themselves from the open air.

Airplane technology changed rapidly during Earhart's flying career. Technology is the application of knowledge in a certain area—in this case, aviation. Earhart kept up with the science.

By the end of her career, she was flying in closed-cockpit planes. She had a radio and a navigator onboard. These airplanes could fly much farther and faster than the earlier planes.

One of Earhart's first planes was a Lockheed Vega. The Smithsonian Institution now owns it. It is displayed in the museum's Pioneers of Flight gallery. Here are some facts about the plane.

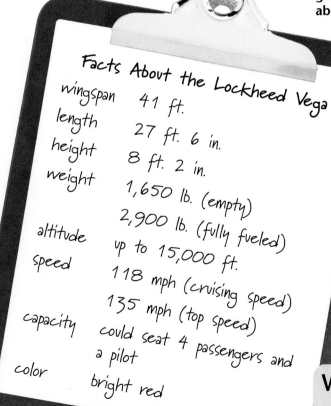

Facts About the Lockheed Vega

wingspan	41 ft.
length	27 ft. 6 in.
height	8 ft. 2 in.
weight	1,650 lb. (empty)
	2,900 lb. (fully fueled)
altitude	up to 15,000 ft.
speed	118 mph (cruising speed)
	135 mph (top speed)
capacity	could seat 4 passengers and a pilot
color	bright red

Vo•cab•u•lar•y

fragile (fraj•uhl)—easily broken or destroyed

Aviation Excitement

Flying by itself wasn't enough for Earhart. She wanted to set and break records. One after another, she set new goals for herself. And she met them. Many of her records were women's records.

Then as now, most airplane pilots were men. Earhart opened up the field of aviation for women. She set records and wrote books about her adventures. She was well known around the world.

She also gave hope to people around the world. They were suffering through the hard **economic** times of the **Great Depression**. They liked hearing about Earhart on the radio. They read about her in the newspaper.

Setting Records

What records did Earhart set? Her first record was set in 1928. She became the first woman to fly across the Atlantic Ocean as a passenger. That same year, however, she also set a record as a pilot. She became the first woman to make a **solo** round-trip flight across the United States.

The mayor of New York City (inset) awards Amelia Earhart a medal following a parade (above) in her honor.

Vo·cab·u·lar·y

economic (ek•uh•**nom**•ik)— related to money and finances

Great Depression—the hard times in the 1930s when many people were out of work

solo (**soh**•loh)—by oneself; in aviation, a flight with only the pilot in the plane

Earhart speaks with reporters following her record-breaking transcontinental flight.

Strategy

Interact With Text by identifying how the text is organized.

Write notes on your own paper to tell how you used this strategy.

In 1929, she came in third in the very first Women's Air Derby. In 1930, she set a women's speed record. She flew 181.19 miles an hour!

In 1932, Earhart became the first woman to fly solo across the Atlantic Ocean. In 1933, she broke her own **transcontinental** record. She flew the coast-to-coast distance in 17 hours, 7 minutes, and 39 seconds. That seems slow today. But for the 1930s it was a very fast trip.

Some of Earhart's records were records for men and women. In 1935, she was the first person to fly over the Pacific Ocean from Hawaii to California. Also that year, she was the first to fly from Los Angeles to Mexico City, Mexico, and from Mexico City to Newark, New Jersey.

What Happened to Earhart?

In 1937, Earhart set off in search of yet another goal. She wanted to fly all the way around the world. She planned to stay as close to the equator as possible.

Vo•cab•u•lar•y

transcontinental (trans•kon•tuh•**nen**•tl)— from one side of a continent to the other

[**171**]

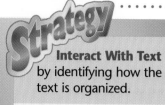

Interact With Text
by identifying how the text is organized.

Write notes on your own paper to tell how you used this strategy.

By this time, Earhart was famous. News reporters and photographers tracked every part of her journey. People around the world were watching and listening to stories about Earhart's trip.

On May 20, 1937, Earhart and her **navigator,** Fred Noonan, took off from Oakland, California. They were flying east. Their route was well planned. There were many stops for rest and refueling.

On July 2, they were flying from New Guinea to Howland Island in the Pacific. Earhart radioed her position. Then she was never heard from again.

Her plane may have crashed into the ocean and sunk. Or it may have been lost forever in a dense jungle on an island. No one knows. Legends have kept on about her disappearance. There have been many reports of sightings of the wreckage of her plane. But neither her plane nor her body has ever been found.

Vo•**cab**•u•lar•y

navigator
(**nav**•i•gay•tuhr)—the crew member who is in charge of keeping the plane on course

Dare to Dream

Do you have a dream? Is there something you want to do? You want it so much that nothing will slow you down? It's easy to focus on Earhart's daring. But she worked hard, too, in following her dream.

She said, "If you find something that you want to do, then do it. If you want to try a certain job, try it. . . . It may turn out to be fun, and fun is an important part of work."

Dreams take work, courage, and the willingness to take risks. Amelia Earhart's life was a mix of all of these. The events surrounding her disappearance are still a mystery. But her spirit lives on in anyone who dares to dream.

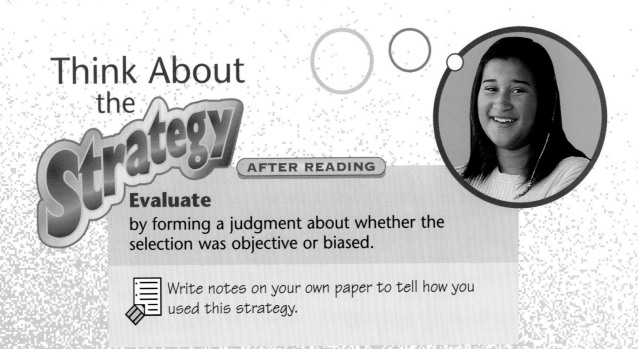

Think About the Strategy

AFTER READING

Evaluate by forming a judgment about whether the selection was objective or biased.

Write notes on your own paper to tell how you used this strategy.

Words Inside Words

Words in English are sometimes made of small words and word parts put together. The **words inside** a long word often relate to the meaning of the long word. For example, the word *personal* contains the word *person*. *Personal* means "private, or having to do with one *person* only." Look for words inside words to help find the meanings of long words.

Reread this passage from "Earhart's Adventures":

> *In 1932, Earhart became the first woman to fly solo across the Atlantic Ocean. In 1933, she broke her own* **transcontinental** *record.*

The word *transcontinental* contains the smaller word *continental,* as well as the prefix *trans*.

> *trans + continental = transcontinental*

The prefix and base word can help you understand what *transcontinental* means. The word *continental* refers to a continent, in this case North America, where the United States is located. The prefix *trans* means "across." When you put the two meanings together, you know that *transcontinental* means "across, or crossing, the continent."

Copy the following words from the selection on a separate sheet of paper. Underline the smaller, inside word or words. Try to find the meaning of the longer word by thinking about the meaning of the inside words. Write your guess for each word's meaning. Check your answers in a dictionary.

1. landing
2. photographer
3. reporters
4. refueling
5. disappearance

6. application
7. newspaper
8. willingness
9. surrounding
10. mysteriously

Journal Entry

When she was 23 years old, Amelia Earhart flew in an airplane for the first time. The following is a fictional journal entry of that ride. The experience changed her life. She fell in love with flight. Practice reading this entry until you are ready to read it aloud to others.

Remember to read with expression. For example, show excitement when you read a sentence that ends with an exclamation point. Remember, an exclamation always ends with an exclamation point (!).

My First Time in an Airplane

December 28, 1920

Today I was a passenger in an airplane! And now I know what it's like to be a bird. The roads and hills are new and different when you look down on them from above. The world will never again look the same to me.

I can feel that this has been a most important day for me. I believe I have found my passion! I must learn to be a pilot. I want to control this powerful machine. I know I had set out to become a doctor. After today, I am not so sure.

I have always felt that I will do something special with my life. That is why I wanted to go to medical school. If I can be an accomplished pilot, I will show women around the world that they, too, are capable of flight. Other women might be inspired to pursue their dreams. Yes, today I have found my dream. I shall take flying lessons. I shall become a pilot.

Think About
the
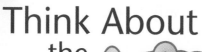
Strategies

BEFORE READING

Activate Prior Knowledge

by reading the introduction and/or summary to decide what I know about this topic.

DURING READING

Interact With Text

by identifying how the text is organized.

AFTER READING

Evaluate

by forming a judgment about whether the selection was objective or biased.

 Use your own paper to jot notes to apply these Before, During, and After Reading Strategies. In this selection, you will choose when to stop, think, and respond.

Pole Position

Roald Amundsen

Robert Scott

Introduction

In 1911, a great international contest took place. Two expeditions raced to be the first humans ever to reach the South Pole. One team was **British,** led by Robert Scott. The other team was a group of **Norwegians**. Whose flag would be planted at that **frigid,** forbidding spot?

The story of the Norwegian team centers on the expert planning of Roald Amundsen [**roh**•ahl **ah**•muhnd•suhn]. Amundsen was an experienced **polar** explorer. He became the leader of the Norwegian group.

A Way of Life

How did the race to the poles begin? The Norwegian group's journey to the South Pole did not begin at a base camp. Nor did it start on the day they set sail from Norway. It began with Amundsen. He had a lifelong **urge** to explore, discover, and compete.

Vo•**cab**•u•lar•y

British (**brit**•ish)—from the country of Great Britain

Norwegians (nor•**wee**•juhnz) —people from the country of Norway

frigid (**frij**•id)—very, very cold

polar (**poh**•luhr)—having to do with Earth's North or South Pole

urge (urj)—a continuing desire to do some particular thing

Amundsen was born in 1872. He grew up in Oslo, Norway. His family owned a fleet of ships. He spent his childhood learning about ships and sailing. He heard stories of faraway places. When Amundsen was away from the water, he spent time snow skiing.

Norway is located far north of the equator. It is snowy and icy much of the time. In those conditions, cross-country skiing is a necessity as well as a sport. Amundsen became a strong skier. These two things—ships and skis—figured in all of Amundsen's adult **endeavors**.

Roald Amundsen's vessel

Dreams of Polar Exploration

Amundsen dreamed of exploring the poles. How did his choices lead toward that goal? He learned as much as he could. In 1894, he went on his first sea voyage in the northern Arctic Sea. He worked as a mate aboard a ship called the *Magdelena*.

On that journey and many others, he gathered information. He also gained physical strength. He studied how the **Inuit** and other people **indigenous** to cold regions lived. He learned about their sleds and dogs.

Vo·cab·u·lar·y

endeavors (en•**dev**•uhrz)—serious, determined efforts

Inuit (**in**•yoo•it)—the people native to the Arctic

indigenous (in•**dij**•uh•nuhs)—having always lived in a place

In 1896, Amundsen made his first long journey to the Antarctic. This is the region surrounding the South Pole. Serving on a ship called the *Belgica* [bel•**jee**•kah], he learned everything he could. He had many conversations with another expedition member, Frederick Cook.

What were some of the things Amundsen learned? He learned how equipment and fur clothing worked in polar conditions. Part of the *Belgica*'s mission was to become frozen in the ice on purpose for several months. Amundsen learned about the physical, mental, and nutritional needs of people under those conditions. He learned how to prevent scurvy. That is a disease caused by a lack of certain vitamins in the diet. And, being Amundsen, he filed the information away for the day he would need it.

Change of Poles

What do you think Amundsen did next? He selected the North Pole as his target. As Amundsen was planning this expedition, though, he heard something. He learned that the North Pole had been reached.

In secret, Amundsen changed his plans. He decided to try for the South Pole instead. The secrecy was important. Another expedition, Scott's, was also heading for the South Pole. Amundsen did not want to speed them up with the news that they had a race on their hands.

The South Pole is the southern end of the earth's axis.

Race to the Pole

Amundsen's expedition arrived in Antarctica in 1911. The team was aboard a ship called the *Fram*. The expedition included just 18 men. They all were experienced sled-dog drivers and skiers. They set up a base camp during January and February. This is during the Antarctic summer.

From the base camp, the team set up food and supply stations. They made sure they were easy distances apart. The stations lined the route they would follow to the Pole. These reserves of hidden food were one of the most important parts of Amundsen's plan.

Robert Scott prepares for his expedition.

Why was food so important to Amundsen? He made sure lots of food was there because he had seen hunger aboard the *Belgica*. He did not want to see it again. On the way to the Pole, the team traveling with dog sleds would leave food behind. They would eat it on the return trip.

Amundsen's rival, Scott, took ponies instead of sled dogs. His team carried all of the food. Amundsen took dogs. He knew they were used to the frozen conditions they would face.

Who made the better choice? Amundsen did. All of Scott's ponies died. His party ended up hauling their sleds by hand.

The Long Winter

Amundsen's team worked as hard as they could during the short summer. As it got colder and darker, they moved inside. They built sleds and checked equipment. They made flags to mark their food reserves. They were trapped in camp by the weather until October 1911.

Finally, Amundsen picked four men. They would make the run to the Pole with him. On October 11, they set out with the dog sleds. They left food in well-marked spots as they traveled.

Average Monthly Temperatures at the South Pole			
Jan.	-18.8*	July	-75.5
Feb.	-41.6	Aug.	-76.0
Mar.	-65.2	Sept.	-74.9
Apr.	-71.1	Oct.	-60.0
May	-70.6	Nov.	-36.9
June	-72.4	Dec.	-17.5

*Note: Temperatures are in degrees Fahrenheit.

Reaching the Pole First

The team traveled from a camp on the Ross Ice Shelf. They went due south to the Axel Heiberg Glacier [**ak**•suhl **hy**•burg **glay**•shuhr]. They climbed the glacier. They came out onto a **plateau**. Travel on the bumpy plateau was difficult. The team was slowed by fog and blizzards. Soon, however, they reached a smoother area.

By December 8, they were farther south than anyone had ever been before. Would they make it to the Pole? Would they beat Scott's expedition?

At 3:00 PM on December 14, 1911, all of their instruments showed that they were there. The team had made it to the South Pole. They looked around carefully and took extra readings. They could find no sign that anyone else had ever been there. They were the first. They had beaten Robert Scott to the Pole!

Excitedly, they planted a flag and took pictures. They pitched a tent for Scott to find and left a letter for him. They asked him to tell the king of Norway about their success if they did not survive the journey back to camp. On December 18, they headed home to base camp. Everyone made it back in good health.

What happened to Scott? Scott and the 4 members of his team had run out of food. Their ponies were dead. They reached the South Pole 34 days after Amundsen. Sadly, Scott and the men with him all died during the return trip from the South Pole.

The Norwegian expedition reaches the South Pole.

Sad Return Home

Amundsen's team left Antarctica on the *Fram* on January 30, 1912. Amundsen went on to lead and partici-pate in many other expeditions. A century later, people remember Scott. But they cannot recall Amundsen's name.

He became the first person to see both the North and the South Poles. (But he only flew over the North Pole.) His thoroughness and planning always served him well.

Sadly, he died in a plane crash at sea in 1928. He was trying to rescue a friend.

Vo•**cab**•u•lar•y

plateau (pla•**toh**)—a wide, flat area of land

Word Roots: *ped*

Many words in English come from Latin **roots**. Knowing the meaning of its root can help you find the meaning of the whole word. The root *ped* comes from the Latin word *pede,* which means "foot."

This passage from the selection "Pole Position" contains a word with the root *ped*. Think about how the meaning "foot" relates to the meaning of the whole word.

> *Amundsen's expedition arrived in Antarctica in 1911. The team was aboard a ship called the* Fram.

Expedition means: "a long journey for a special purpose, such as exploring." In the past, people on expeditions traveled by foot.

Look at other words and their meanings that come from the root *ped*:

pedestrian, which means "someone who travels on foot"

pedal, which means "a lever on a bicycle, car, or piano, for example, that you push with your foot"

centipede, which means "a small creature with a very long body and many legs"

biped, which means "an animal with two feet"

pedestal, which means "a kind of foot, base, or support upon which something rests"

On a separate sheet of paper, write one or more sentences using each word. Remember, they are defined above. Show in each sentence that you understand the meaning of the word.

1. expedition
2. pedestrian
3. pedal
4. centipede
5. biped
6. pedestal

Acrostic Poem

The following is an acrostic poem. The first letter of each line, when read vertically, spells "Amundsen." Practice reading this poem several times until you can read it smoothly. When you are ready, perform it for the class.

Fluency TIP

Remember to read slowly, clearly, and with expression.

Roald Amundsen, Explorer

Roald Amundsen was born in 1872.

Oslo was where he learned sailing and skiing, too.

All his life he dreamed of exploring the Poles.

Learning a lot would help him reach his goals.

Daring and brave, he left for the Antarctic.

Amundsen studied what people needed to not get sick.

Making secret plans, he headed for the South Pole.

Unlucky Scott thought the race was under his control.

Not wanting to starve, Roald buried and hid food.

Dogs pulling the sleds also made his journey good.

Secrecy he maintained as he pursued his goal.

English explorer Scott failed to beat him there.

No competition was too much. Roald won fair and square.

Table

Here is a list showing the highest peak in each state of the United States. Study the table, and then answer the questions on the next page.

State	High Point	Feet	State	High Point	Feet
Alaska	Mount McKinley	20,320	Vermont	Mount Mansfield	4,393
California	Mount Whitney	14,494	Kentucky	Black Mountain	4,145
Colorado	Mount Elbert	14,433	Kansas	Mount Sunflower	4,039
Washington	Mount Rainier	14,410	South Carolina	Sassafras Mountain	3,560
Wyoming	Gannett Peak	13,804	North Dakota	White Butte	3,506
Hawaii	Mauna Kea	13,796	Massachusetts	Mount Greylock	3,491
Utah	Kings Peak	13,528	Maryland	Backbone Mountain	3,360
New Mexico	Wheeler Peak	13,161	Pennsylvania	Mount Davis	3,213
Nevada	Boundary Peak	13,143	Arkansas	Magazine Mountain	2,753
Montana	Granite Peak	12,799	Alabama	Cheaha Mountain	2,407
Idaho	Borah Peak	12,662	Connecticut	Mount Frissell	2,380
Arizona	Humphreys Peak	12,633	Minnesota	Eagle Mountain	2,301
Oregon	Mount Hood	11,239	Michigan	Mount Arvon	1,979
Texas	Guadalupe Peak	8,749	Wisconsin	Timm Hill	1,951
South Dakota	Harney Peak	7,242	New Jersey	High Point	1,803
North Carolina	Mount Mitchell	6,684	Missouri	Taum Sauk Mountain	1,772
Tennessee	Clingmans Dome	6,643	Iowa	High Point	1,670
New Hampshire	Mount Washington	6,288	Ohio	Campbell Hill	1,550
Virginia	Mount Rogers	5,729	Indiana	High Point	1,257
Nebraska	Mount Constable	5,426	Illinois	Charles Mound	1,235
New York	Mount Marcy	5,344	Rhode Island	Jerimoth Hill	812
Maine	Mount Katahdin	5,268	Mississippi	Woodall Mountain	806
Oklahoma	Black Mesa	4,973	Louisiana	Driskell Mountain	535
West Virginia	Spruce Knob	4,863	Delaware	Tower Hill	448
Georgia	Brasstown Bald	4,784	Florida	Britton Hill	345

Discussion Questions

Answer these questions with a partner or on a separate sheet of paper.

1. What is the highest peak in your state?

2. Mount St. Helens is a famous mountain in Washington State. Why isn't it on this list?

3. Which of these mountains is higher than Mount Hood in Oregon?
   a. Guadalupe Peak in Texas
   b. Mount Washington in New Hampshire
   c. Wheeler Peak in New Mexico
   d. Mount Mitchell in North Carolina

4. Are any mountains in Hawaii higher than Mount Elbert in Colorado? Explain your answer.

5. Are all the mountains in Alaska higher than all the mountains in California?
   a. Yes, because Alaska comes before California on this list.
   b. Yes, because Mount McKinley in Alaska is higher than all the mountains in the United States.
   c. No. Only Mount McKinley is higher than all the mountains in California.
   d. No. Some mountains in Alaska are smaller than some mountains in California.

6. Will the mountain peaks on this list change from year to year?
   a. Yes, the list will change as new mountains are discovered.
   b. Maybe the list will change, as measuring techniques become more accurate.
   c. Maybe the list will change, as some peaks become more popular with vacationers.
   d. No, because mountains never change.

7. Do you think Driskell Mountain in Louisiana should be called a mountain? Give reasons for your answer.

8. What does this chart tell you about the highest mountains in the main part of the United States?
   a. Most of the highest mountains are in the West.
   b. Most of the highest mountains are in the Southeast.
   c. Most of the highest mountains are on the coasts.
   d. Most of the highest mountains are near the Great Lakes.

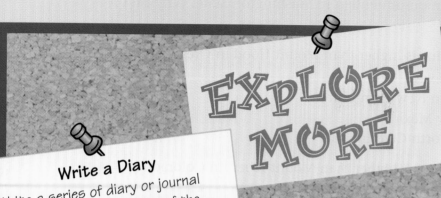

Write a Diary

Write a series of diary or journal entries describing what one of the Sherpa guides may have thought, felt, and experienced as he participated in the momentous and historic climb up Mount Everest with Hillary and Norgay.

Choose a Race

Explore a modern endurance race, such as the Iditarod, the America's Cup, the Tour de France, or another race of your choosing. Gather information, and prepare a report, either oral or written, or a display of the race you choose.

Make a Report

Gather information about another early aviator or explorer, such as Charles Lindbergh, George Mallory, Robert Peary, Bessie Coleman, Jacques Cousteau, Louise Boyd, or another of your choosing. Prepare a written, oral, or visual presentation of the person and his or her most famous or notable achievements.

Meet an Explorer

Imagine that you have an opportunity to meet and talk with one of the explorers presented in this unit. What is one important question you would like to ask that person? Write a journal entry or a magazine article that describes your meeting. Tell the main ideas the two of you discussed. Be sure to include supporting details.

Get a Job!

Think of a job you might like to do that involves travel . Research the requirements for the job, the places you might be traveling to, and what you will be doing when you get there. Present your information in the form of a written or oral report or as a bulletin board display.

Go Exploring

Think of a place that you would like to explore. Write a description of what and where the place is, how you plan to get there, and what special preparations you have to make in order to make the trip. You might want to include drawings or illustrations.

Related Books

Brennan, Kristine. *Sir Edmund Hillary: Modern-Day Explorer*. Chelsea House Publishers, 2001.

Calvert, Patricia. *Sir Ernest Shackleton: By Endurance We Conquer*. Benchmark Books, 2003.

Coburn, Broughton. *Triumph on Everest: A Photobiography of Sir Edmund Hillary*. National Geographic Society, 2000.

Connolly, Sean. *Amelia Earhart: An Unauthorized Biography*. Heinemann Library, 2001.

Dickinson, Matt. *Everest: Triumph and Tragedy on the World's Highest Peak*. HarperCollins, 2002.

Green, Jen. *You Wouldn't Want to Be a Polar Explorer! An Expedition You'd Rather Not Go On*. Franklin Watts, 2001.

Hooper, Meredith. *Antarctic Adventure: Exploring the Frozen South*. DK Publishing, Inc., 2000.

Jerome, Kate Boehm. *Who Was Amelia Earhart?* Grosset & Dunlap, 2002.

Loves, June. *The People*. Chelsea House Publishers, 2003.

Masoff, Joy. *Everest: Reaching for the Sky*. Scholastic Inc., 2002.

McLeese, Don. *Amelia Earhart: Discover the Life of an American Legend*. Rourke Publishing LLC, 2003.

McLoone, Margo. *Women Explorers of the Air: Harriet Quimby, Bessie Coleman, Amelia Earhart, Beryl Markham, Jacqueline Cochran*. Capstone Books, 2000.

Pflueger, Lynda. *Amelia Earhart: Legend of Flight*. Enslow Publishers, Inc., 2003.

Raatma, Lucia. *Amelia Earhart*. World Almanac Library, 2001.

Riddle, John. *Robert Scott*. Mason Crest Publishers, Inc., 2003.

Roop, Connie, and Peter Roop. *Escape From the Ice: Shackleton and the Endurance*. Scholastic Inc., 2001.

Salkeld, Audrey. *Mystery on Everest: A Photobiography of George Mallory*. National Geographic Society, 2000.

Schaefer, Lola M. *Amelia Earhart*. Capstone Press, 2003.

White, Matt. *Endurance: Shipwreck and Survival on a Sea of Ice*. Capstone Press, 2002.

Interesting Web Sites

http://www.ellensplace.net/eae_intr.html
http://www.south-pole.com/
http://www.achievement.org/autodoc/page/hil0pro-1?rand=1231
http://www.pbs.org/wgbh/nova/everest/
http://imagingeverest.rgs.org/Concepts/Virtual_Everest/
http://www.ameliaearhart.com/
http://www.pbs.org/wgbh/nova/vinson/
http://www.achievement.org/autodoc/page/hil0bio-1

Unit 6 Strategies

BEFORE READING

Set a Purpose

by skimming the selection to decide what I want to know about this subject.

DURING READING

Clarify Understanding

by deciding whether the information I'm reading is fact or opinion.

AFTER READING

Respond

by forming my own opinion about what I've read.

LEARN
the strategies
in the selection
Bulldoggin' Bill
page 191

U.S. MAIL

PRACTICE
the strategies
in the selection
The Story of Stagecoach Mary
page 203

APPLY
the strategies
in the selection
Riding for the Pony Express
page 211

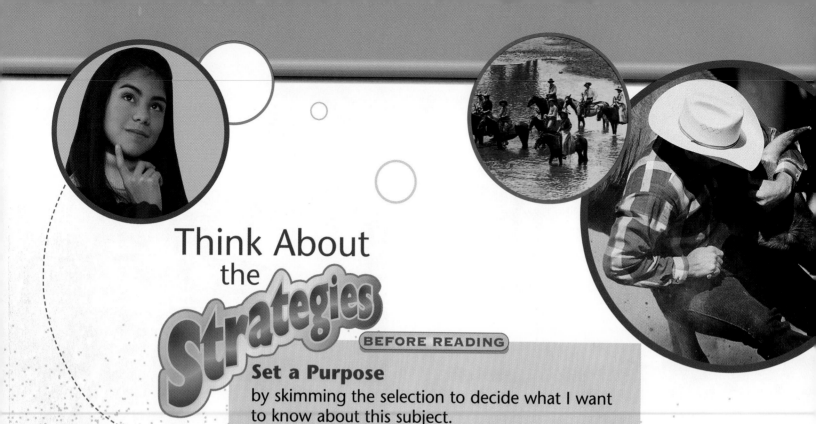

Think About
the
Strategies

Set a Purpose

by skimming the selection to decide what I want to know about this subject.

My Thinking

The strategy says to set a purpose by skimming the selection to decide what I want to know about this subject. To skim, I'll look at the pictures, headings, and boldface words. The pictures and photos all have people that look like cowboys and have something to do with cowboys. I see that some of the headings talk about an arena, rodeos, steer wrestling, and cowboys. I think I want to know more about who Bulldoggin' Bill was and how he was involved with cowboys. Now I'm ready to read and find out.

Clarify Understanding

by deciding whether the information I'm reading is fact or opinion.

My Thinking

The strategy says to clarify understanding by deciding whether the information I'm reading is fact or opinion. I will stop and think about this strategy every time I come to a red button like this ⦿.

Bulldoggin' Bill

Bulldoggin' Bill waved his hat at the cheering audience.

"**Lay-deez** and gentlemen, give a big Texas welcome to that bulldoggin' wizard of the West. Here's Bill Pickett, the **Dusky** Demon!" The rodeo announcer's voice boomed. The crowd cheered. A gate opened at one end of the arena, and out rode Bill Pickett on his best horse **Spradley**. The crowd continued to hoot and holler as Pickett trotted around the arena, waving his big old cowboy hat at the people who had come to see him.

Vo•cab•u•lar•y

lay-deez—ladies

dusky (**duhs**•kee)—dark, as in the evening

Spradley (**sprad**•lee)—Bill Pickett's horse

[191]

People had come to see him. How did that happen? He was just a ranch hand who grew up selling vegetables. How did this crowd of people come to be cheering for him, an African American cowboy whose parents had been slaves?

Action in the Arena

But this was no time for thinking. It was time for action. Another gate opened. A huge bull with angry eyes and big, sharp-pointed horns came thundering into the arena. Pickett and Spradley knew just what to do. They galloped around in a curve. They came up alongside the bull. Horse hooves and bull hooves thundered in the dirt. They drowned out the sound of the crowd in Pickett's ears. As the horse and bull matched **strides,** Pickett took a leap into the air. He leaped across the space between his horse and the bull, landing right on the bull's back! The **furious** bull snorted and bucked.

Pickett wrapped his arms around the bull's horns, twisting its head back until he and the bull were face to face. Then he sank his teeth right into the bull's upper lip! The bull was so shocked that he dropped to the ground. The people in the crowd went crazy. Bill Pickett had done it again. He had wrestled a bull and won! ⬤

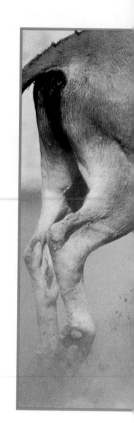

Life and Times of the Rodeo

Nobody thought up rodeos. They began in the late 1800s. They started out as **informal** contests among cowboys. Other cowboys were the only audience. Gradually these contests became events. People from surrounding farms and towns would hear about the cowboys' skills and come out to watch. Cowboys would "pass the hat," and the **spectators** would toss in a few coins for the winners.

Then somebody thought of charging people to watch. Some cowboys were so good that they were able to earn a living as rodeo riders. That's how the rodeo was born. Today rodeos travel all over the world. They entertain millions of people.

Vo•cab•u•lar•y

strides (strydz)—steps, or lengths of steps

furious (fyur•ee•uhs)—very angry

informal (in•for•muhl)—casual, not organized

spectators (spek•tay•tuhrz)—people who are watching

Steer Wrestling

Bulldogging is the rodeo event that made Bill Pickett famous. He invented it. One day he saw a bulldog bring down a cow by biting and holding onto its lip. The cow stopped struggling instantly when its lip was bit. Young Pickett just had to try it, too!

Bulldogging, or **steer** wrestling, as it is now called, is one of the seven events in professional rodeos. (The other six are saddle bronc riding, bareback riding, bull riding, calf roping, team roping, and barrel racing.) ⬤·········

A cowboy wrestling a steer at a rodeo

Strategy

Clarify Understanding by deciding whether the information I'm reading is fact or opinion.

My Thinking
Well, this all sounds like what might go on in a rodeo. And the list of rodeo events seems real. I think this part of the article is factual.

Bill Pickett Invitational Rodeo
2003 Tour Through Atlanta
Bulldoggin' Event

	Contestant	Points
1.	Clarence LeBlanc	2,717.67
2.	Anthony Thorton	2,645.09
3.	Kenneth LeBlanc	2,007.16
4.	Reuben Haynes	1,960.80
5.	Brother Gilder	1,872.51
6.	Wefus Tyus	1,783.81
7.	Jesse Guillory	1,352.32
8.	Ben Goodman	1,340.51
9.	Donald Goodman	848.03
10.	Alfred Ousley	724.47

Vo·cab·u·lar·y

steer—in cattle, a male animal not able to produce young

[193]

Life and Times of Bill Pickett

Bill Pickett was born somewhere near Austin, Texas, around 1870. No one knows the exact date or place of his birth. The West was still pretty wild then. People didn't take time to stop and keep records. Pickett's father, Thomas, had come to Texas from South Carolina in the 1850s. He was a slave and had to go where his **master** went.

In 1865, however, slavery ended for all African Americans. Thomas Pickett was free. He met Mary Gilbert. They married, bought a piece of land, and began raising a family. Bill Pickett was the second of their 13 children.

The family farmed and sold their crops of vegetables. But young Bill could never seem to pay any attention to farming. He was more interested in cowboys. His family lived near one of the main trails for taking cattle to market. Groups of cowboys would ride by. They were **herding** thousands of cattle along the trail in what was called a cattle drive. The cow that the bulldog bit was probably from one of these herds.

A cattle drive

Becoming a Cowboy

Pickett had a deep interest in cowboys. He also had uncles who were cowboys. So, it's no surprise that when he was 15 years old, Pickett set out on a cowboy career of his own. There were many African American cowboys in the Old West. Many had moved west with former masters. They stayed after they became free, like Thomas Pickett.

Other African Americans had moved west on their own. They hoped to take advantage of the opportunities that were not open to them back east. Good workers were valuable. Most ranchers didn't make decisions based on the color of someone's skin. If you were a good worker, you had a job.

Vo·cab·u·lar·y

master (**mas**•tuhr)—someone who has control or ownership over another

herding (**hurd**•ing)—moving animals in a group

Rodeo Years

Pickett worked as a cowboy and ranch hand off and on. But his skill as a bulldogger soon gave him a new career. Wherever Pickett was working, people would come around to watch him wrestle steers to the ground. Soon he began performing in rodeos and shows. In time, he became a full-time rodeo rider.

One day, the owner of a huge ranch, the 101 Ranch in Oklahoma, hired Pickett to tour with his rodeo. It was the famous 101 Ranch Wild West Show. Bill Pickett and Spradley became the stars of the show.

Pickett traveled all over the world with the 101 Ranch Wild West Show. But in 1916 he went home. He was tired. He wanted to spend time with his family. He never stopped working with horses though. And he kept in good bulldoggin' shape. Sadly, in 1932, a wild horse on the 101 Ranch in Oklahoma kicked him. He died from those injuries.

Strategy

Clarify Understanding by deciding whether the information I'm reading is fact or opinion.

My Thinking
Real photographs go along with what the selection is saying. This helps me decide that the information I'm reading is fact.

Cowboys in early Oklahoma

The Hall of Fame

In 1971, Pickett was **inducted** into the National Cowboy **Hall of Fame** and Western **Heritage** Center. The center is in Oklahoma City. He is now listed in the Rodeo Hall of Fame of this museum. That's good. That means his life and his deeds—and his bulldoggin'—will live on for a good long time. Bill Pickett, the Dusky Demon, and his horse Spradley will be remembered for years to come. ◉

This picture of Bill Pickett is from a movie poster. Bill starred in *The Bull-Dogger,* in 1922.

Vo·cab·u·lar·y

inducted (in·**duk**·tid)— placed

hall of fame—a place that honors famous people in a certain field and displays pictures and items they used during their lives

heritage (**her**·i·tij)—things shared from the past

In the mid-1980s, the Bill Pickett Invitational Rodeo was set up. Its organizers wanted to honor Bill Pickett and his part in the early American rodeo. They also wanted to call attention to the role of African Americans in the history of the Old West. The Bill Pickett Invitational Rodeo is an all-black rodeo that travels around the U.S. Fans remember the famous man who helped open the door to a lasting part of American history.

Think About the Strategy

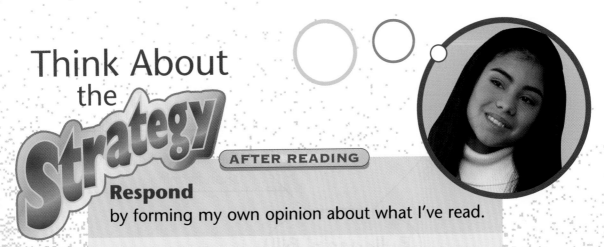

AFTER READING

Respond
by forming my own opinion about what I've read.

My Thinking
The strategy says that I should respond by forming my own opinion about what I've read. That means I need to decide what I think about the article. Well, based on what I've read in school and in library books and what I've seen in movies, I think this selection is fact. The photographs and captions help me know for sure that the information in the article is fact.

Graphic organizers help us to organize information we read. I think this text can be organized by using a spider map. Here is how I organized the information. I put my central idea in the middle. I used main ideas for the legs of the spider. Then I put details about the ideas on the lines coming out from the legs.

Spider Map

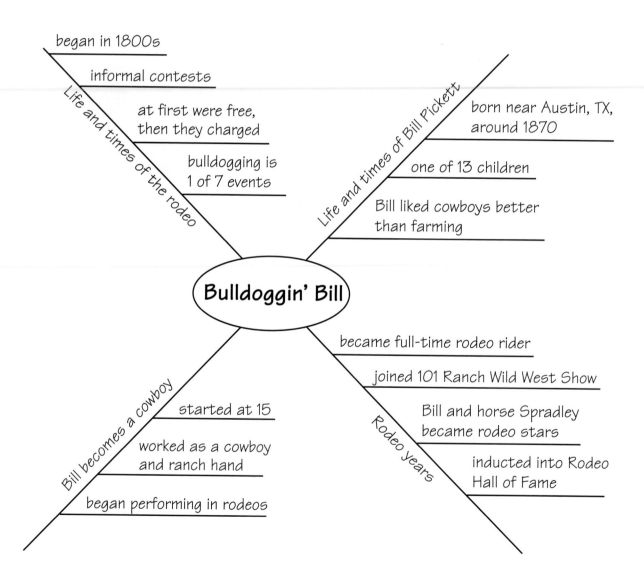

Life and times of the rodeo
- began in 1800s
- informal contests
- at first were free, then they charged
- bulldogging is 1 of 7 events

Life and times of Bill Pickett
- born near Austin, TX, around 1870
- one of 13 children
- Bill liked cowboys better than farming

Bulldoggin' Bill

Bill becomes a cowboy
- started at 15
- worked as a cowboy and ranch hand
- began performing in rodeos

Rodeo years
- became full-time rodeo rider
- joined 101 Ranch Wild West Show
- Bill and horse Spradley became rodeo stars
- inducted into Rodeo Hall of Fame

I used my graphic organizer to write a summary of the article. Can you find the information in my summary that came from my spider map?

A Summary of
Bulldoggin' Bill

Have you ever watched a rodeo? Rodeos started in the late 1800s. The first ones were just contests between cowboys. Other cowboys watched—for free. Later, rodeos were more organized. People had to pay to see them. Now millions of people go to see rodeos. There are seven main events. One is steer wrestling. It's also called bulldogging.

The most famous bulldogger was Bill Pickett. Pickett was born near Austin, Texas, around 1870. He was one of 13 children. His father had been a slave. Pickett grew up on a farm. Still, he wanted to be a cowboy, not a farmer.

When Pickett was 15, he became a cowboy and ranch hand. He learned how to wrestle steers. Soon he started performing in rodeos.

Then Pickett decided to work for rodeos full-time. He joined the 101 Ranch Wild West Show. He and his horse, Spradley, became famous. Pickett retired in 1916 and died in 1932. Now he is in the Rodeo Hall of Fame.

Introduction
Here is my introduction. It tells what I will write about. The main idea is in the center of my spider map.

Body
I used information from each leg of the spider map for the paragraphs in my body copy.

Conclusion
I concluded my paper by telling about things that happened late in Bill's life and after his death.

The Prefix *in-*

A **prefix** is a word part that comes at the beginning of a word. A prefix changes the meaning of a word. Knowing the meaning of a prefix can help you find the meaning of a whole word. For example, the prefix *in-*, when added to an adjective, means "not."

As you read this passage from the selection "Bulldoggin' Bill," think about the meaning of the word in boldface with the prefix *in-*.

> Nobody thought up rodeos. They began in the late 1800s. They started out as **informal** contests among cowboys. Other cowboys were the only audience. Gradually these contests became events.

To find the meaning of *informal,* divide the word into its parts:

Prefix	+	Root	=	Word
in-	+	*formal*	=	*informal*

Formal is an adjective that means "official or organized." Therefore *informal* means "not formal" or "casual, not organized."

Other words with *in-* are *inactive, invisible,* and *indirect.* When you divide each word into its parts, you can tell that *inactive* means "not moving," *indivisible* means "not able to be divided," and *indirect* means "not in a straightforward way."

Write each of the following adjectives on a separate sheet of paper. Draw a line to divide each adjective into its two main parts: a prefix and a root. Then write the definition that matches the adjective. Use a dictionary if you need help.

in- Words
1. inappropriate
2. inaudible
3. incomplete
4. inexpensive
5. insufficient

Word Meanings
a. not loud enough to be heard
b. not enough
c. not costing a lot of money
d. not correct for the time or place
e. not finished or complete

Readers' Theater

Janie is a big fan of Bill Pickett, so Uncle Bob took
Janie to the Wild West Show. The following is a script
of what they might have said as they watched the
show. Practice reading the script with a partner. When
you are both ready, perform the script for the class.

As you read, remember to be expressive. Think
about the characters' personalities when you
read each part.

At the Wild West Show

Janie: This is so exciting, Uncle Bob! Thank you so much for
bringing me to see the famous 101 Ranch Wild West Show. I
can't wait to see Bill Pickett in action!

Uncle Bob: Sure, Janie. I'm excited to see him, too. But I still
don't see how you came to admire Bill Pickett so much!

Janie: Oh, I love Bill Pickett. He invented steer wrestling.
Imagine taking on a bull! He's strong, and he's not afraid of
anything. That's just how I plan to be when I grow up.

Uncle Bob: Surely you're not going to start bulldoggin' at a
rodeo, Janie?

Janie: Maybe I will! I bet when Bill was growing up picking
vegetables, no one ever thought he'd turn out to be the best
rodeo cowboy around. Maybe the same will be true of me. Sure
I'm a girl, but I can do whatever I set my mind to!

Uncle Bob: You sure are your mother's daughter, Janie. She is
the most determined person I've ever known. Even still, you
should start out slow by roping calves.

Janie: Will you teach me, Uncle Bob?

Uncle Bob: Well, I'd like to keep my eye on you and teach you
the skills you need to be safe around bulls. Then we can talk
about bulldoggin' . . . . Here comes Bill Pickett! That poor bull
doesn't have a chance.

Janie: Go, Bill! You're the best!

Think About
the
Strategies

Set a Purpose

by skimming the selection to decide what I want to know about this subject.

 Write notes on your own paper to tell how you used this strategy.

DURING READING

Clarify Understanding

by deciding whether the information I'm reading is fact or opinion.

 When you come to a red button like this ⦿, write notes on your own paper to tell how you used this strategy.

The Story of Stagecoach Mary

Back when I was a girl, around the early 1900s, there was a woman in our town like no one I had ever met before. And in all the long years I've lived, I've never met another like her. She was very old when I was a child. And she was famous in our town, which was Cascade, Montana. Her name was Mary Fields. We called her "Stagecoach Mary."

Just Mary Fields

Mary Fields was so famous in Cascade that her birthday was a holiday. We always got the day off from school. That was reason enough to like her. But no one really knew when Mary's birthday was. One year we celebrated it twice! Stagecoach Mary did lots of things no one had ever seen a woman do before. And she did them well. Mary did exactly what she wanted to do. Nobody messed with Mary.

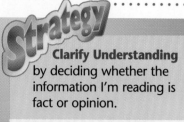

Tennessee Times

Stagecoach Mary was born in Tennessee in 1832. She was born into slavery. No one knows much about her early years. And somewhere along the way she learned other skills that made her famous. She had the ability to shoot straight, drive a team of horses, work hard, and keep her word. And somewhere along the way, she grew to be 6 feet tall, the tallest woman I ever saw, and 200 pounds strong. But she wasn't Stagecoach Mary, yet.

Montana Move

In 1865, African Americans were given their freedom, including Mary. Somehow, she made her way north to Toledo, Ohio. She was working there for a Catholic nun in 1881. The nun, Mother Amadeus [ah•muh•**day**•uhs], was asked to move from Toledo to St. Peter's **Mission**. This was 8 miles outside of Cascade, Montana.

A few years later, Mother Amadeus wrote to Mary back in Toledo. She offered her a job hauling supplies and doing heavy work for the mission. Mary Fields took her up on the offer. In 1884, she moved to Montana. She was still just Mary Fields, but not for long.

Mary and the Wolves

For eight years, Mary worked for a school called St. Peter's Mission. She drove wagons loaded with supplies back and forth between the mission and the town. She smoked a big cigar and carried a rifle and a pistol. Nothing was going to happen to the supplies while Mary was in charge.

My folks told me the story of Mary and the wolves. It was a dark, dark night. Mary was late getting back to St. Peter's. Nearby, she heard howling. Then, she heard growling. Suddenly, a blur of gray—several blurs of gray—came flying out of the bushes. Wolves! The horses **shied and reared** and broke their **traces**. Off they went, galloping to safety. The wagon tipped, spilling bags, boxes, and barrels onto the road.

But what about Mary? Mary was quick. She fired the pistol and then the rifle, frightening the wolves back a few

Vo•cab•u•lar•y

mission (**mish**•uhn)—a Christian church set up to minister to nonmembers

shied and reared—in horses, backed up with the front legs in the air

traces (**tray**•suhz)—the parts of a harness that attach a horse to a wagon

yards. Quickly, she gathered **sagebrush** from the sides of the road. She lit a blazing fire to keep the wolves away.

When the town was just waking up, in came Mary. She had loaded the supplies back onto the wagon and came **trudging** to the school, hauling that wagon herself. She was stubborn, and she was strong. She made sure no wolves would get her supplies.

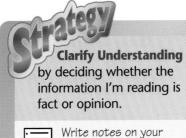

Strategy

Clarify Understanding by deciding whether the information I'm reading is fact or opinion.

Write notes on your own paper to tell how you used this strategy.

Stagecoach Mary at Last

Mary was friendly—unless she was crossed. She had many adventures and did things no one had ever seen a woman do before. She became a **legend** around Cascade. The bishop up at Helena, Montana, started hearing things about her, good and bad. One day, she had an argument with one of the workers at the school. She challenged him to a shoot-out. Well, that was too much for the bishop. Mary was out of a job.

For a while, she ran a restaurant, but it went out of business fast. Mary kept giving away food. She couldn't turn away anyone who was hungry. Meanwhile, she got the job that gave her the nickname that stuck. She got a job driving the town's stagecoach. In 1895, in her sixties, Mary Fields finally became Stagecoach Mary.

A stagecoach was a closed wagon with seats inside. It was pulled by four or more horses. Stagecoaches carried people, supplies, and the mail. Stagecoach Mary was only the second woman in the United States to carry the mail. And she was the first African American woman to do it. Whether people liked Mary or not didn't matter.

Vo·cab·u·lar·y

sagebrush (sayj•brush)— a shrubby plant that grows in the western plains

trudging (truh•jing)— walking with slow, heavy steps

legend (lej•uhnd)— someone who is popular for reasons that may or may not be true

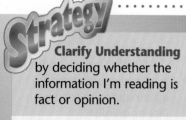

Strategy

Clarify Understanding by deciding whether the information I'm reading is fact or opinion.

Write notes on your own paper to tell how you used this strategy.

What mattered was that she could be trusted with important letters and packages. If anyone could get the mail through, it was Stagecoach Mary Fields.

Stagecoach Mary's Laundry

When Stagecoach Mary was in her seventies, she started yet another career. She felt too old to drive, so she started a laundry business. That's what she was doing when I was a child. I remember the day she knocked out a customer. He hadn't paid for his laundry, and that made Mary angry.

One day, when she was at the hotel, she saw him pass by. She went right outside and knocked him out cold with her fist. When she came back inside, she said, "Well, that bill's settled." That was one of the last stories about Mary. She died in 1914.

Stagecoach Mary's Legend

Stagecoach Mary lives on in legend now, but she was a real, flesh-and-blood woman. You can still see her grave in the Hillside Cemetery in Cascade. At least you could see it the last time I was there. The town loved her. The hotel gave her all her meals free. And when the laundry burned down, the whole town pitched in with free **lumber** and free labor. She was back in business in no time.

For a long time, a **portrait** of her hung in one of the banks in Cascade. Every time I saw it, I smiled. Stagecoach Mary was tough. She lived life exactly the way she wanted to. She didn't worry about what people thought of her. But do you know what they thought of her? They thought she was a great woman.

Vo•cab•u•lar•y

lumber (**lum**•buhr)—wood that has been sawed into boards

portrait (**por**•trit)— a painting of a person

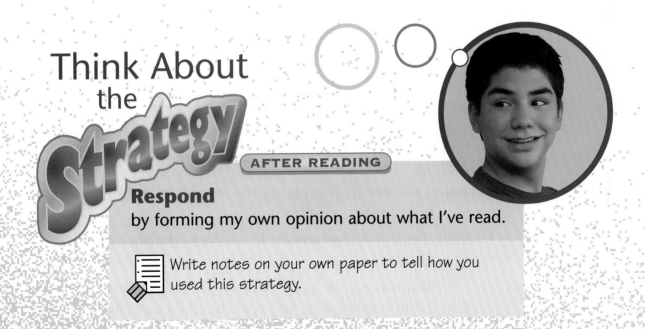

Think About the Strategy

AFTER READING

Respond

by forming my own opinion about what I've read.

Write notes on your own paper to tell how you used this strategy.

Vocabulary

Context Clues

When you are reading and come to a new word, look at the words near the new word. Then look at the sentences nearby. There are often clues called **context clues** in the sentence and surrounding sentences that can help you find the meaning of a new word. Read the following sentence from the selection "The Story of Stagecoach Mary."

*Stagecoach Mary lives on in **legend** now, but she was a real, flesh-and-blood woman.*

Try to find the meaning of the word *legend* by looking for context clues. What things or ideas in the sentence might be related to the word? The first clue is the phrase *lives on*. The phrase tells you that she is remembered, probably through the stories about her. The second clues are *real, flesh-and-blood woman*. The second phrase suggests that not all *legends* or stories are about real people. Together the clues suggest that *legend* means "a story that is handed down from the past and may or may not be true."

Read the following sentences from the selection. On a separate sheet of paper, write each word in boldface. Then write the context clues in the sentence that can help you figure out the meaning of the word. Then write the word's meaning. Check your answers in a dictionary.

1. Mary Fields was so **famous** in Cascade that her birthday was a holiday.

2. And somewhere along the way she learned other **skills** that made her famous. She had the ability to shoot straight, drive a team of horses, work hard, and keep her word.

3. The horses shied and reared and broke their **traces**. Off they went, galloping to safety.

4. I remember the day she knocked out a **customer**. He hadn't paid for his laundry, and that made Mary angry.

5. For a long time, a **portrait** of her hung in one of the banks in Cascade. Every time I saw it, I smiled. Stagecoach Mary was tough.

Poetry

Read the following poem about Stagecoach Mary aloud to your-self until you can read it with expression. When you are ready, perform the poem for a partner.

Remember to pay attention to the rhythm of the poem. Use the punctuation to help you decide when to pause.

Stagecoach Mary

Stagecoach Mary was a legend
　　known for feats of strength and might.
She weighed at least two hundred pounds
　　and stood six feet in height.

She could haul loads like no one else,

Drove her wagon with the supplies.

The people of Cascade all knew

She would never tell a lie.

When Mary drove her wagon to the mission one day,

Wolves scared the horses, causing them to run away.

Mary quickly lit some brush on fire,

To make those wolves back down.

She soon loaded up the wagon

And pulled it back to town.

How did Mary get her nickname? I was wondering
　　the same.
Born as Mary Fields, but "Stagecoach" Mary
　　brought her fame.
She drove the small town's stagecoach,

People, goods, and even mail.

Known to be reliable,

She arrived through wind or hail.

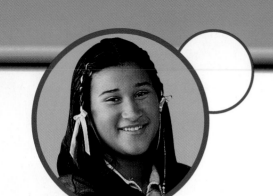

Think About
the
Strategies

BEFORE READING

Set a Purpose
by skimming the selection to decide what I want to know about this subject.

DURING READING

Clarify Understanding
by deciding whether the information I'm reading is fact or opinion.

AFTER READING

Respond
by forming my own opinion about what I've read.

 Use your own paper to jot notes to apply these Before, During, and After Reading Strategies. In this selection, you will choose when to stop, think, and respond.

Riding for the Pony Express

Wanted:

*Young,
skinny,
wiry fellows
not over 18.*

**Must be expert riders
willing to risk death daily.**

ORPHANS PREFERRED

Wages: $25.00 a week.

Who would want a job like that? What kind of company would ask its employees to risk death? Read on to learn why hundreds of young men wanted this job. You will find out why only 80 riders were chosen and what they were asked to do. You will also learn how they became legends in only 18 months!

The Need for News

By the spring of 1860, half a million people were living in the new states of Oregon and California. They had traveled there by horse, mule, covered wagon, and stagecoach. There were no airplanes and no cars. Train tracks went no farther than the Missouri River. The first tracks to cross the nation would not be ready for nine years.

Most of the people living on the West Coast had gone there hoping to find gold. But they still wanted to stay in touch with their families back East. They had also heard rumors about a possible civil war. They were desperate for news.

Yet they had no televisions, radios, or telephones. Telegraph lines could send messages long distances by **Morse code**. But like the train tracks, these lines stopped at the Missouri River. People could send letters from one coast to the other on ships. But the trip all the way around South America often took six months!

This postage stamp shows a Pony Express rider and a map of the 2,000-mile route.

Making Promises

Sending mail overland seemed like a better idea. Starting in 1858, Congress paid a stagecoach company. It was to carry mail between St. Louis, Missouri, and Sacramento, California. The long route curved south through Texas and New Mexico.

The stagecoaches made the 2,800-mile trip twice a month. The trip took three weeks each way. That was much faster than sending mail on a ship. But people did not want to wait even that long for news.

William Russell had two partners. The group had run a successful **freight** company for years. The company used wooden wagons pulled by oxen. The wagons carried tons of materials across the Great Plains and the Rocky Mountains. In 1860, Russell talked his partners into starting a new company. They started the Pony Express.

Riders on speedy horses would carry mail and news overland. Russell and his partners decided on a route. It was different from the one the stagecoaches took. The riders would travel straight west. This route would be "only" 2,000 miles long. But it crossed the Sierra Nevada Mountains.

Vo·cab·u·lar·y

Morse code (mors kohd)— a way of sending messages using a system in which letters and numbers are represented by dots and dashes or long and short signals

freight (frayt)—goods carried by vessel or vehicle

The owners knew this route would be difficult in winter. Still, Russell promised that their riders could deliver mail in ten days. Even his partners were not sure they could meet that goal.

Getting Started

The new company needed riders and horses. Hundreds of young men answered the advertisement you read earlier. But Russell and his partners chose only 80 of the best riders. They picked small, strong, brave men. Few of them weighed over 120 pounds. A heavy man would slow down his horse.

The average horse then cost about $50. But the Pony Express did not want average horses. At the eastern end of the route, the company paid up to $200 for a horse. Like the men, the horses had to be small, strong, and brave. Short legs would help them on the slippery mountain slopes.

Station keepers cared for the horses and made sure they were ready for the next rider. They were paid about $50–$100 a month.

At the western end of the route, many of the horses were mustangs. Mustangs are wild horses. They are known for their strength, speed, and intelligence. They were caught for the Pony Express. But there was no time for taming and training. For some horses, the first person to sit on their backs was the Pony Express rider. The first part of his ride was like a rodeo. The mustang often tried to buck the rider off!

The Pony Express bought about 500 horses. They lived in **stables** at 120 **stations** along the route. When it was time for a rider to come by, the station man got a fresh horse ready. The rider would jump off his sweaty horse and onto the fresh one. This switch might take only 15 seconds. The rider also moved the mail pouch, called a **mochila,** to his new horse.

Vo•cab•u•lar•y

stables (**stay•**buhlz)— buildings used to house horses

stations (**stay•**shuhnz)— stopping places along the route of the Pony Express

mochila (moh•**chee•**luh)— a leather bag used by the riders to carry the mail

Then the rider would take off at a **gallop**. He stopped for nothing. Seconds counted in the tight schedule. After riding about 15 miles, he came to another station. There, he changed horses again. Each rider changed horses 5 to 7 times. He rode 75 to 100 miles. Then he passed the mochila to the next rider.

Riding Into History

The Pony Express ran 24 hours a day. The tough riders were able to complete the 2,000-mile route in 10 days or less. They galloped across burning deserts. They picked their way through icy mountain passes. Often they had to outrun robbers. The robbers knew the mail might contain gold or money.

At first, Pony Express riders were paid $80 a month. Later, many earned about $100–$125 a month.

In addition, Native Americans often chased riders who crossed their land. One rider was shot in the forehead with an arrow, but he survived! "Willing to risk death daily" was truly part of the job. Yet only one man died while riding for the Pony Express.

The riders quickly became heroes. Crowds cheered them as they galloped through towns. People liked to tell about one rider who was only 14 years old. One day, robbers trapped him in a canyon. One robber reached for the mochila. The rider grabbed the other end and threw it at the robber's face. The rider escaped with his life and the mail. His name was Billy Cody. Now he is known as Buffalo Bill Cody.

Another time, Cody pulled his sweating horse to a stop at a station. They had just traveled 116 miles. But Cody learned that the next rider had died the night before. He jumped onto a fresh horse. They carried the mail another 76 miles to the next station. There, a fresh rider took over. Cody headed back to his home station. He rode 384 miles, stopping only to change horses.

The horse of another rider, George Little, died. It was in a fierce snowstorm. Little stuffed the mail into his shirt. Then he walked to Salt Lake City. He was 16 years old at the time. Stories like these are part of the legend of the Pony Express.

The End of the Ride

On October 24, 1861, the first telegram was sent from San Francisco to Washington, D.C. Crews in Salt Lake City had just connected telegraph wires. The wires linked both coasts.

Two days later, the Pony Express closed. There was no longer a need for it. News traveled much faster by telegraph. Sadly, the Pony Express had been losing money during its entire 18-month run. Russell and his partners were broke.

The riders had galloped 600,000 miles. They had carried 34,752 pieces of mail. And they had helped make the West Coast part of our new nation.

The United States had many challenges ahead as it entered the Civil War. However, the daring riders of the Pony Express helped build a nation that could meet those challenges.

Eponyms

An **eponym** is a word that comes from the name of a person. Many eponyms come from the names of inventors. Others come from the names of people who behaved a certain way or who were the first to do something special. Read this sentence from "Riding for the Pony Express":

> *Telegraph lines could send messages long distances by* **Morse code.**

Morse code is "a way of sending messages using a system in which letters and numbers are represented by dots and dashes or long and short signals." It is named after Samuel Morse, who invented the telegraph in 1835. Morse code was first used to send telegraph messages.

Look for the eponym in this sentence:

> *At the school for the blind, there is a large library of Braille books.*

If you said that the eponym is the word *Braille,* you are right. *Braille* is a system of raised dots that allows blind people to read with their fingers. It is named after the Frenchman who invented it, Louis Braille.

Match the eponym on the left with its definition and origin on the right. Write your answers on a separate sheet of paper.

1. sandwich
2. boycott
3. diesel
4. saxophone
5. leotard

a. to refuse to buy something or to take part in something as a way of making a protest; Charles Boycott, a real estate agent who was shunned in 1880 by Irish farmers renting land

b. a fuel used in certain engines; Rudolf Diesel, who built the first successful engine to use this kind of fuel

c. a wind instrument made of brass; Adolphe Sax, who invented the instrument in the 1840s

d. a tight, one-piece garment worn for dancing or exercise; Julius Leotard, a 19th-century French aerial gymnast

e. two or more pieces of bread around a filling; John Montagu, 4th Earl of Sandwich, who is said to have invented this food

Advertisement

The following is what an advertisement might have looked like for the Pony Express. It might have been printed on sheets of paper and posted around a main street, or it might have appeared in a newspaper. Testimonials are included in the advertisement. A testimonial is a customer's opinion of a product or service. When you are ready, read the advertisement to the class.

Read this ad the first time as if you really believe in the Pony Express. Then read it as though you think the idea will never work. Change your voice and expression to show your feelings each time.

USE THE PONY EXPRESS

TEN DAYS OR LESS WITH THE PONY EXPRESS!

Do you have news that needs to get somewhere fast?

USE THE PONY EXPRESS

Feeling out of touch with your friends and family?

USE THE PONY EXPRESS

Want to do business with people back East?

USE THE PONY EXPRESS

"I'm starting a business, and I need to send news to my investors back East. With Pony Express, I never worry about my mail arriving months later. Those riders are the best!"
—*Bill Friend, Portland*

"It used to take six months for my letters to reach my brother in New York. And then it would be another six months before I'd hear back from him. With the Pony Express, he gets my letter in two weeks!" —*Jacob Shale, San Francisco*

Sequence

How a Bulldogger Wrestles a Steer

Steer wrestling takes courage and strength. The steer weighs up to half a ton. Here is how the bulldogger does it. After reading this page, answer the questions on the next page.

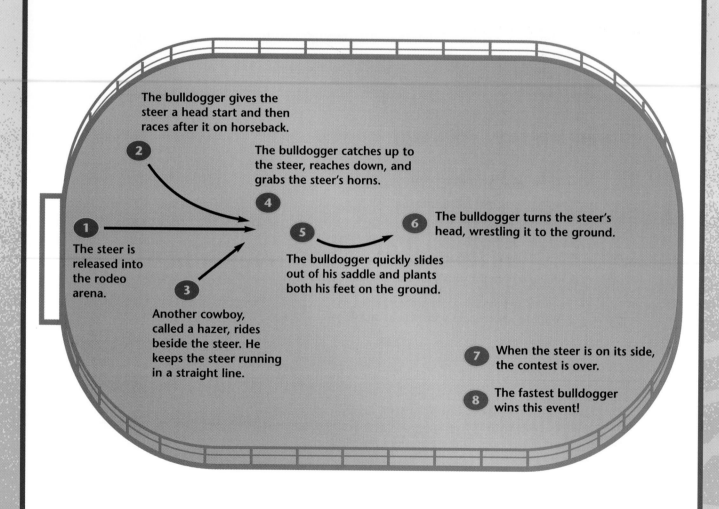

2 The bulldogger gives the steer a head start and then races after it on horseback.

4 The bulldogger catches up to the steer, reaches down, and grabs the steer's horns.

1 The steer is released into the rodeo arena.

6 The bulldogger turns the steer's head, wrestling it to the ground.

5 The bulldogger quickly slides out of his saddle and plants both his feet on the ground.

3 Another cowboy, called a hazer, rides beside the steer. He keeps the steer running in a straight line.

7 When the steer is on its side, the contest is over.

8 The fastest bulldogger wins this event!

Discussion Questions

Answer these questions with a partner or on a separate sheet of paper.

1. During the bulldogging event, how many cowboys are in the arena with the steer?

2. What happens after the bulldogger catches up with the steer?
   a. He plants both feet on the ground.
   b. He turns the steer on its side.
   c. He grabs the steer's horns.
   d. He slides out of his saddle.

3. What is the hazer's job?
   a. to give the steer a head start into the arena
   b. to catch up with the steer
   c. to distract the steer from the cowboy
   d. to keep the steer running in a straight line

4. What might happen if the hazer did not do his job?
   a. The steer might dart in different directions.
   b. The steer might stop running.
   c. The steer might run too fast.
   d. The bulldogger might fall off his horse.

5. How do the rodeo judges decide who wins the bulldogging event?

6. Why does bulldogging require strength?

7. Who do you think is braver, the bulldogger or the hazer? Explain your answer.

8. Why do you think bulldogging was invented?
   a. to win money in rodeo events
   b. to stop steers who were running away
   c. to show how brave a cowboy was
   d. to entertain people at rodeos

CONNECTING
to the Real World

EXPLORE MORE

Rodeos

Work with a partner or a small group to gather information and prepare a collage or other visual display presenting photos, drawings, facts, and interesting things to know about modern rodeos and rodeo stars.

Your Life as a Rider

Pretend you are a rider for the Pony Express. Write a series of diary entries describing your experience. Be sure to include information about what you see, think, feel, hear, and experience.

Interview Mary

Imagine being a reporter interviewing an elderly Stagecoach Mary. With a partner or a small group, develop a list of questions you would ask her. Have one person pretend to be Mary. Carry out the interview as a live presentation, or prepare an audiotape or videotape version of it.

Write a Story

Choose one of the people presented in this unit, and write a fictional story about that person in a new situation. The story could be in the form of a tall tale, a play, a newspaper article, an "autobiography," or another form of your choosing.

Write a Poem

Choose a person from one of the articles in this unit, and write a poem or a song about that person. Include interesting bits of information and facts about the person and his or her life and experiences. You might want to present your poem or song to the class as a performance.

Write a Brief Report

Choose a topic covered in one of the selections in this unit and write a brief report. The report could be from a historical standpoint, in which you relate information additional to what was in the article. Or it might be a focus from modern times that includes aspects of what you learned in one of the articles. If possible, add photos or pictures to enhance your report.

Related Books

Anderson, Peter. *The Pony Express.* Children's Press, 1996.

De Angelis, Gina. *The Black Cowboys.* Chelsea House Publishers, 1998.

Dolan, Edward F. *The Pony Express.* Benchmark Books, 2003.

Hanes, Bailey C. *Bill Pickett, Bulldogger: The Biography of a Black Cowboy.* University of Oklahoma Press, 1989.

Katz, William Loren. *Black Pioneers: An Untold Story.* Atheneum Books for Young Readers, 1999.

—*Black Women of the Old West.* Atheneum Books for Young Readers, 1995.

Lilly, Melinda. *The Pony Express.* Rourke Publishing LLC, 2003.

McCormick, Anita Louise. *The Pony Express in American History.* Enslow Publishers, Inc., 2001.

Pinkney, Andrea Davis. *Bill Pickett: Rodeo-Ridin' Cowboy.* Harcourt Brace & Co., 1996.

Riddle, John. *The Pony Express.* Mason Crest Publishers, 2003.

Sanford, William R., and Carl R. Green. *Bill Pickett: African-American Rodeo Star.* Enslow Publishers, Inc., 1997.

Van der Linde, Laurel. *The Pony Express.* New Discovery Books, 1993.

Wukovits, John. *The Black Cowboys.* Chelsea House Publishers, 1997.

Yancey, Diane. *Life on the Pony Express.* Lucent Books, Inc., 2001.

Interesting Web Sites

Here are sites to visit to learn more about the people and history presented in this unit.

http://www.billpickettrodeo.com

http://www.xphomestation.com

http://social.chass.ncsu.edu/slatta/essays/blackcowboys.htm

http://www.ponyexpress.org/index.htm

http://www.reggaecowboys.com/reggaecountry.html

http://www.lkwdpl.org/wihohio/fiel-mar.htm

http://library.thinkquest.org/10320/Pickett.htm